Smart Cities in Europe
Open Data in a Smart Mobility Context

Maria SASHINSKAYA

Brussels, 2014

Abstract: The process of urbanization continues to increase. In order to make fast growing cities more comfortable for living, local authorities are taking actions. One of the popular attempts is to make the urban area "smarter". As a result, public sector information (PSI) and Open Data are becoming raw material and one of the basics of Smart Cities. The book is based on previous academic research work of the author and discusses the issues of "Smart Cities" and "Smart Mobility" as well as the role of PSI in the European Union. The major aim of this book is to explore how the concept of "Smart Mobility" can be practically implemented and how city data can play its role. The empirical part of the book covers the case studies of three European capitals: London, Berlin and Brussels.

Key words: Smart Cities; Smart Mobility; Public Sector Information; Open Data; Policy Analysis; Case Studies.

Smart Cities in Europe: Open Data in a Smart Mobility context
Copyright © 2014 Maria SASHINSKAYA
All rights reserved.

ISBN-13: 978-1522924890
ISBN-10: 1522924892

Acknowledgments

Many thanks to:

Prof. Dr. Pieter Ballon, for growing an academic motivation and fostering a personal interest in the "Smart Cities" domain.

Nils Walravens *(iMinds-SMIT)* for the friendly guidance and constructive criticism.

Andrew Stott *(World Bank/UK Transparency Board)*, **Pieter Colpaert** *(The Open Knowledge Foundation)*, **Pieter Van Ostaeyen** *(De Lijn)* for the long and inspiring conversations.

Hans Van Mingroot *(IBM Belux)* and **Corinna Schulze** *(IBM CHQ, Governmental Programs)* for giving me the opportunity to put my knowledge into practice.

My family for the emotional support and strong belief.

Table of Contents

INTRODUCTION	9
PART 1. THEORETICAL FRAMEWORK	13
CHAPTER 1: SMART CITIES CONCEPT	13
SMART CITY CLASSIFICATIONS	16
SMART CITY AS A CONNECTED CITY	17
SMART CITY AS A CREATIVE CITY	19
SMART CITY AS AN ENTREPRENEURIAL CITY	21
BASIC COMPONENTS OF A SMART CITY	26
CITY (GOVERNMENT) AS A PLATFORM	34
SUMMARY AND CONCLUSIONS	36
CHAPTER 2: SMART MOBILITY IN THE CONTEXT OF URBAN MOBILITY	39
CLASSICAL URBAN MOBILITY	39
"SMART" URBAN MOBILITY	44
ROLE OF DATA IN THE "SMART MOBILITY" CONCEPT	47
AN OVERVIEW OF THE EU INITIATIVES ON SMART MOBILITY	51
SUMMARY AND CONCLUSIONS	54
CHAPTER 3: OPEN DATA CONCEPT IN A DISCOURSE OF SMART CITIES	56
WHAT IS OPEN DATA?	56
GIVING DEFINITIONS TO OPEN DATA	61
OPEN DATA CLASSIFICATION	64
WHAT IS REAL "OPENNESS"?	68
GOVERNMENTAL MOTIVATIONS TO OPEN-UP ITS DATA	72
CRITICS OF OPEN DATA CONCEPT	77
SUMMARY AND CONCLUSIONS	84
CHAPTER 4: OPEN DATA. THE LEGAL FRAMEWORK OVERVIEW	86
INTERNATIONAL FRAMEWORK. OECD - PRINCIPLES AND GUIDELINES FOR ACCESS TO RESEARCH DATA FROM PUBLIC FUNDING (2007)	87
EUROPEAN UNION FRAMEWORK.	90
DIGITAL AGENDA AND PUBLIC DATA CORE DIRECTIVES	90
DIRECTIVE 2003/98/EC OF THE EUROPEAN PARLIAMENT AND	

OF THE COUNCIL ON THE RE-USE OF PUBLIC SECTOR INFORMATION (OF 17 NOVEMBER 2003 93
DIRECTIVE 2007/2/EC OF THE EUROPEAN PARLIAMENT AND OF THE COUNCIL ESTABLISHING AN INFRASTRUCTURE FOR SPATIAL INFORMATION IN THE EUROPEAN COMMUNITY (INSPIRE) (OF 14 MARCH 2007) 104
CORRESPONDENCE OF TWO DIRECTIVES 108
SUMMARY AND CONCLUSIONS 109
PART 2: EMPIRICAL RESEARCH 111
CHAPTER 5: CASE STUDIES LONDON, BERLIN, BRUSSELS 111
MOTIVATION OF CHOICE AND RESEARCH METHODOLOGY 111
CASE STUDY №1. CITY OF LONDON 113
THE PUBLIC TRANSPORT SYSTEM 113
LEGISLATIVE FRAMEWORK 115
PSI DIRECTIVE IMPLEMENTATION 115
INSPIRE DIRECTIVE IMPLEMENTATION 117
"OPEN DATA WHITE PAPER" 121
OVERVIEW OF APPLICATIONS FOR URBAN MOBILITY IN THE CITY OF LONDON 125
CASE STUDY №2. BERLIN 136
THE PUBLIC TRANSPORT SYSTEM 136
LEGISLATIVE FRAMEWORK 138
PSI DIRECTIVE IMPLEMENTATION 138
INSPIRE DIRECTIVE IMPLEMENTATION 142
OVERVIEW OF APPLICATIONS FOR URBAN MOBILITY IN BERLIN 146
CASE STUDY №3. BRUSSELS 156
THE PUBLIC TRANSPORT SYSTEM 156
LEGISLATIVE FRAMEWORK 158
PSI AND INSPIRE DIRECTIVES IMPLEMENTATION 158
OVERVIEW OF APPLICATIONS FOR URBAN MOBILITY IN THE CITY OF BRUSSELS 160
OPEN DATA INITIATIVE IN BELGIUM 160

OVERVIEW OF APPLICATIONS	**168**
FINAL CASES CONCLUSIONS	**175**
CONCLUSIONS AND FUTURE WORK	**179**
RECOMMENDATIONS	**185**
EPILOG	**189**
ABOUT THE AUTHOR	**191**
BIBLIOGRAPHY	**192**

Introduction

"Faced with demographic ageing and global competition we have three options: work harder, work longer or work smarter. We will probably have to do all three, but the third option is the only way to guarantee increasing standards of life for Europeans".

A Digital Agenda for Europe, 2010 [1]

According to the latest international statistics, more and more people around the globe are moving to urban areas to live[2]. The population of world megapolises is significantly increasing. As a result, cities face a variety of urban problems such as bad ecology, insufficient transportation, high unemployment statistics, increasing criminal activity rates and others. Many local authorities are making steps towards

---

[1] EUROPEAN COMMISSION. COM (2010) 245 final.
Communication from the Commission to the European Parliament, the Council, the European Economic and Social Committee and the Committee of the Regions, a Digital Agenda for Europe. 19.5.2010. Available online: http://eur-lex.europa.eu/LexUriServ/LexUriServ.do?uri=COM:2010:0245:FIN:EN:PDF (Last retrieved 15/09/2012)

[2] The United Nations (2011) "The State of World Population 2011 Report", *the United Nations Population Fund.* . Available online: http://foweb.unfpa.org/SWP2011/reports/EN-SWOP2011-FINAL.pdf (Last retrieved 15/09/2012)

resolving these issues in a traditional manner: urban development programs, policy regulation, penalty measures etc. Some of the governments are making an extra step by developing an idea to make a city "smarter". It is a trendy approach in order to adapt the urban reality to the citizen's demands with the help of ICT.

The aim of this book is to look critically at the possibilities for a city to become mobile and comfortable for its citizens. It is a broad topic and this is why we narrowed down our research on the "Smart Mobility" issues, primarily focusing on the public sector information and open data ideas development in the European Union scale.

The main questions are:

1. *What is "Smart Mobility" in a modern urban space?*
2. *How can the concept of "Smart Mobility", based on public sector information and open data, be defined and practically implemented?*

Conceptually, following the academic approach, the book is divided into two essential parts a theoretical and a practical part.

The first, theoretical part, consists of four Chapters,

in which the topics of Smart Cities, Smart urban Mobility functioning and the role of data in these processes are discussed.

In the first Chapter we try to give a definition of a "Smart City" and it's components by analyzing the concepts, given by a range of academic authors and researchers.

The second Chapter focuses on one particular component of a smart city, discussed earlier – the "Smart Mobility". The aim of the second Chapter is to define factors making a city more mobile and perform better. Particularly we are looking at the ICT and data exploitation impact on the process of urban mobility.

Chapter 3 is a logical extension of the previous Chapter. In this piece of paper we discuss the broad concept of "Open Data" by reflecting on a notion of "openness", looking at the governmental motivation to open up its data and giving arguments "pro and contra" this recent trend.

Chapter 4 finishes our theoretical overview by mapping the existing international and European Union legislation on the public sector information (PSI) and open data issues. Focusing specifically on the EU policy, we analyze in detail two core Directives on the open data domain.

In the empirical part of our research we start with the case studies research to investigate how the concept of smart mobility can be applied to real life examples. For this purpose we selected three European capitals – London, Berlin and Brussels. Every case is analyzed by the same set of parameters including the local transport system overview, legislative framework (referring to the previous policy analysis Chapter) and urban mobility applications. In the end of the case studies research we compare all three cases on the agreed set of parameters and making the conclusions of how the current urban mobility in the EU functions and what can be improved.

In the final part we try to summarize all the theoretical and empirical results we assembled and we answer the main research questions of the paper: *What is "Smart Mobility" in a modern urban space? How can the concept of "Smart Mobility", based on public sector information and open data, be defined and practically implemented?*

We find the topic of this research relevant in both dimensions: academic and applied. It is obviously a credible advantage that we have a chance to investigate fairly new conceptual and policy domains, supporting it by recent real life examples – the EU case studies.

Part 1. Theoretical framework
Chapter 1: Smart Cities Concept

The last report of the United Nations Population Fund says that around seven billion people inhabit the Earth and about one in two of these people lives in a city. In about 35 years, the population of cities will be even much more increased and two out of three people will be living in urban areas.[3] With the fast growth of the urban population, cities face a variety of problems from ecological and transport issues to unemployment and crime rates increasing. Thus, it's not surprising that local authorities try to find optimal solutions on how make the life of cities' inhabitants more comfortable and safe and at the same time to get benefits out of this urban growing tendency. Basically, there are two possible ways: to make a city bigger, giving citizens a chance to find their place in urban reality or to make a city smarter, adapting urban reality to citizen's demands.

Digital Agenda for Europe is a flagship initiative of the EU which was launched in August 2010 and aimed to develop a digital single market in the territory of the

---

[3] The United Nations (2011) "The State of World Population 2011 Report", *the United Nations Population Fund.* . Available online: *http://foweb.unfpa.org/SWP2011/reports/EN-SWOP2011-FINAL.pdf* (Last retrieved 15/09/2012)

European Union.[4] The main standing point of this initiative is the idea that nowadays public, governmental and commercial services are moving towards more digitalization and the European Union can definitely benefit from this tendency. Therefore, to remain competitive in a the world market during economically challenging periods and at the same time making life of European citizens more comfortable, it is necessary to work on the development of new services. The idea that the European cities should become "smarter" or "more intelligent" is one of the core inspirations of the EU authorities: *"This Digital Agenda does seek to recognize the power of urban planning and the role of ICTs in managing infrastructures"*.[5]

In fact, the idea of a sustainable city is not a new one. We probably can say that the first attempts to make the urban environment more comfortable were made in line with inventions of alternative and renewable energy tools in the

---

[4] EUROPEAN COMMISSION. COM (2010) 245 final. Communication from the Commission to the European Parliament, the Council, the European Economic and Social Committee and the Committee of the Regions, a Digital Agenda for Europe. 19.5.2010. Available online: http://eur-lex.europa.eu/LexUriServ/LexUriServ.do?uri=COM:2010:0245:FIN:EN:PDF (Last retrieved 15/09/2012)

[5] EUROPEAN COMMISSION. COM (2010) 245 final. Communication from the Commission to the European Parliament, the Council, the European Economic and Social Committee and the Committee of the Regions, a Digital Agenda for Europe. 19.5.2010. Available online: http://eur-lex.europa.eu/LexUriServ/LexUriServ.do?uri=COM:2010:0245:FIN:EN:PDF (Last retrieved 15/09/2012)

70's of 20th century. [6] Still the expression "Smart City" is often used referring to smart grids and green energy. Finally, the term has made a shift from sustainable energy matters towards the impact of ICTs usage in urban space (where ICTs can resolve energy issues as well).

To be objective till the end in our research, we definitely should mention one more important issue – the critics on the modern smart cities concept. Hence, the opponents of the concept argue that so-called "intelligent cities" can be the reason for social stratification. Citizens who have internet access, as well as proper digital literacy and brand new gadgets, will be definitely benefiting from smart cities solutions. At the same moment, the rest of the population with lower education and income levels will stay at the same stage of urban problems or even can be cut off. The other complaint of smart cities opponents is that only big IT and digital companies can get profit out of the concept. These companies know how to earn money on a variety of new services and products for smart cities maintenance, while ordinary citizens may not even need all these advanced features, pushed and imposed by big businesses, in their

---

[6] The United Nations (2011) "Technology Roadmap Carbon Capture and Storage in Industrial Applications", UNITED NATIONS INDUSTRIAL DEVELOPMENT ORGANIZATION

everyday life.[7] We think that the critics on the "Smart City" concept as well as all "pros" and "cons" are fair enough as smart city is only a recent concept. Therefore, reflecting on this topic requires a detailed treatment and thus can be only mentioned within a framework of our current research.

Smart City classifications

To make a classification of the modern "Smart Cities" concept, we should clearly indicate the lack of current academic literature on the topic and to acknowledge that because of this issue, it is not very simple to give a precise definition to a smart city and distinguish some list of concrete characteristics which a city should meet to be labeled as a "smart" one. Thus, we will consider and reflect on several conceptions of this recent phenomenon to cover different angles.

Different authors are trying to describe a smart city in different ways: as a *"technologically progressive city"*, *"knowledge*

---

[7] Fioretti, M. (2011)" Open Data: Emerging trends, issues and best practices", *Laboratory of Economics and Management of Scuola Superiore Sant'Anna,* Pisa

economy and entrepreneurial city" or even a *"creative city"*.[8] [9] [10] The purpose of our paper is not to give one clear definition because the topic is still developing, but to focus on some significant characteristics, which can bring all these theories together.

Smart City as a Connected City

The first and the most noticeable tendency among researchers is identifying a smart city as a *digital* or *connected city*.[11] It means that existing technical infrastructure is becoming a determinant for categorizing a city as a smart one. In fact, many authors are talking about technology driven developments and the way ICTs are creating a new world without boundaries.[12]

Such a digital city cannot be imaginable without

---

[8] Schaffers, H. & N. Komninos (2011) "Smart Cities and the Future Internet: Towards Cooperation Frameworks for Open Innovation", *The future Internet*, Springer-Verlag Berlin, pp. 431-446
[9] Komninos, N. (2002) *Intelligent Cities*. London: Spon Press
[10] Hollands, R.G. (2008) Will the real smart city please stand up?. In: *City*, 12(3).
[11] Landry, C (2008) The Creative City: A toolkit for urban innovators, London: Earthscan.
[12] Gibson, D.V., G. Kozmetsky, R.W. Smilor, (1992) *"The Technopolis Phenomenon: Smart Cities, Fast Systems, Global Networks"*. Boston: Rowman and Littlefield Publishers,

embedded systems, sensors and smart meters as well as the population's usage rate of smart phones, tablets, PC and other digital devices should be relatively high.[13] Basically, it means that an intelligent city or region should have a high capacity for technological innovation and development.[14] But does it mean that if a city is wireless or digital it is a smart city by pre definition? Is it true that underground cables and a high connectivity penetration can guarantee a smart urban space? Obviously, we cannot agree that only technologically determined cities with tangible brand new infrastructure have all the conditions for sustainability. Nevertheless, the adoption of information technology infrastructure is a precondition. Thus, modern ICTs should be functional and fit the aims they are supposed to serve: *"Every digital city is not necessarily intelligent, but every intelligent city has digital components...a digital city refers to a connected community with flexible, service-oriented computing infrastructure based on open industry standards; and, innovative services to meet the needs of governments and their employees, citizens and businesses".* [15]

---

[13] Schaffers, H. & N. Komninos (2011) "Smart Cities and the Future Internet: Towards Cooperation Frameworks for Open Innovation", *The future Internet*, Springer-Verlag Berlin, pp. 431-446
[14] Komninos, N. (2002) *Intelligent Cities*. London: Spon Press
[15] Harrison, C. & B. Eckman, R. Hamilton (2010) Foundations for Smarter Cities. *IBM Journal of Research and Development*, 54(4).

Smart City as a Creative City

Nowadays the usage of "smart" mostly refers to an innovations and new technologies driven society, but social factors are also essential to modern urban places. In this sense, some authors demonstrate a socio-technological view on a smart city. The second popular approach in a smart city explanation refers to human innovative urban space and the idea that ICTs together with creative industries can transform city areas economically, socially and spatially.[16]

Landry calls creativity "a new currency", because it's possible to add value to the city through the creation of innovations.[17] The author is not strongly focused on creative industries themselves, but on co-called "creative ecology", which establishes new values and develops assets by creating new services. We can also define a smart creative environment as the one which is able to collect and use knowledge about its citizens to adapt and increase the potential of the user routine.[18] According to Landry, cities

---

[16] Hollands, R.G. (2008) Will the real smart city please stand up?. In: *City*, 12(3).

[17] Landry, C (2008) The Creative City: A toolkit for urban innovators, London: Earthscan.

[18] D. J. Cook & M. Youngblood (2004) "Smart Homes",. Berkshire Encyclopedia of Human-Computer Interaction. Berkshire Publishing Group.

generate problems of growth and development by themselves and creativity is called to resolve it. Creativity in terms of the author is nothing but a capacity based on human capital characteristics, rather than IT itself, which cannot automatically transform and improve urban reality. [19] Other researchers also see a smart city as a space which "...*gives inspiration, shares culture, knowledge, and life, and motivates its inhabitants to create and flourish in their own lives*".[20]

Richard Florida in his book "The Rise of the Creative Class"[21] also thinks about the role of voluntary organizations and knowledge networks. He suggests three basic "T's": *"tolerance", "technology",* and *"talent"* and concluded that it's definitely smart people, who are the most important component of a smart city. According to the author, a creative city is, first of all, a human city, focused on education. Florida believes that the best educated people can be attracted by intelligent cities as magnets. Talents are attracted by economical and social aspects, by the

---

[19] Landry, C (2008) The Creative City: A toolkit for urban innovators, London: Earthscan.
[20] Harrison, C. & B. Eckman, R. Hamilton (2010) Foundations for Smarter Cities. *IBM Journal of Research and Development*, 54(4).
[21] Florida, R. (2002) *The Rise of the Creative Class: And How It's Transforming Work, Leisure, Community and Everyday life.* New York: Basic Books. Available at:
http://www.washingtonmonthly.com/features/2001/0205.florida.html
(Last retrieved 05/08/2012)

opportunity of a place to develop human potential. Smart people definitely benefit from a smart place, but it also works the other way around – places are becoming "more intelligent" if people make an effort to implement their talents and creativity.

On the other hand, such a city can make a possible diversification between those who have IT skills and the rest and generate the question of "inclusion-exclusion"[22] As a smart city concept itself, the question of a social stratification and diversification by principle of access (to knowledge, information, devices, tools etc.) meets a lot of critics among opponents. And a researcher should always keep in mind that the idea of a smart city as a "creative city" as well as "connected city" is not a neutral one and should be further developed.

Smart City as an Entrepreneurial City

The concept of a smart city as an *"entrepreneurial city"* or *"knowledge economy city"* could be a combination of both previous approaches, as long as here technology meets human factors. Again, "entrepreneurial city" in this case is

---

[22] Landry, C (2008) The Creative City: A toolkit for urban innovators, London: Earthscan.

very often considered by authors as a high-tech variation of a city, as a place which is based on ICT technologies as a core of its business. [23]

According to Landry[24], the main aspect of a true smart city is when the use of new technologies is in a line with a strong entrepreneurial state culture. Referring to business innovations as a basis for modern city development, researchers indicate an increasing number of small- and medium sized enterprises (SMEs) and its co-operation and with local government ("3P"-'Public–Private Partnerships') or even more advanced "4P" ecosystems ("Public-Private-People Partnership"), which provide opportunities to citizens and businesses to experiment and co-create together. [25]

Obviously, an entrepreneurial city cannot function properly without governmental support and sufficient policy-making practices, tailored to support innovative environment and the increase its potential. This idea automatically set smart government as an important component of a smart entrepreneurial city. To facilitate smart city initiatives it is

---

[23] Hollands, R.G. (2008) Will the real smart city please stand up?. In: *City*, 12(3).
[24] Landry, C (2008) The Creative City: A toolkit for urban innovators, London: Earthscan.
[25] Schaffers, H. & N. Komninos (2011) "Smart Cities and the Future Internet: Towards Cooperation Frameworks for Open Innovation", *The future Internet*, Springer-Verlag Berlin, pp. 431-446

necessary to establish an administrative environment, integrated and transparent governance, strategic networking and partnerships, which allow interconnecting between citizens, communities and businesses to achieve a real progress.[26] A productive partnership of public and private sector also means that city policy-makers, citizens and local enterprises should not only be interested in big marketing and promotional "smart" projects for a region, they should mainly be focused on real applied innovations which can improve the everyday life of citizens and increase both business creativity and social participation.[27]

Frequently PPP also refers to user driven innovations as a connecting link between networks of businesses and governments.[28] According to the authors, user's participation helps not only to push innovation, but also to increase the quality of existing services, when users can help service developers to improve their products by indicating drawbacks and coming up with some new ideas. In other words, smart or intelligent cities are based on an *"innovation-friendly*

---

[26] California Institute for Smart Communities (2001) Smart Communities Guide Book. Available online: http://www.smartcommunities.org/guidebook.html (Last retrieved 04/08/2012)
[27] Komninos, N. (2002) *Intelligent Cities.* London: Spon Press
[28] Schaffers, H. & N. Komninos (2011) "Smart Cities and the Future Internet: Towards Cooperation Frameworks for Open Innovation", *The future Internet*, Springer-Verlag Berlin, pp. 431-446

environment", which is clearly supported by the local community. [29] Moreover, PPP initiatives are aimed to attract external sources of funding, new investments and potential employment resources. [30] Thus, support of government and policy for governance is a fundamental condition for designing and implementing smart initiatives: *"Smart communities is about institutions, where government and citizens are partners with a help of IT"* [31]

The Initiative of a smart government should be directed not only to smart business' increasing needs, but also to smart citizens' new demands. An intelligent city is focused on user-oriented participation and intended to solve their problems. [32] As a basis of a smart city, smart governance means an engagement of citizens in decision-making and public/social services development: *"At the most fundamental level, smarter government means making operations and services truly*

---

[29] Komninos, N. (2002) *Intelligent Cities*. London: Spon Press.
[30] Harvey, D. (1989) *From Managerialism to Entrepreneurialism: The Transformation in Urban Governance in Late Capitalism*, Geografiska Annaler. Series B, Human Geography, 71(1), The Roots of Geographical Change: 1973 to the Present, pp. 3-17.
[31] California Institute for Smart Communities (2001) Smart Communities Guide Book. Available online: http://www.smartcommunities.org/guidebook.html (Last retrieved 04/08/2012)
[32] Lorsignol, F. & Y. Sheri (2011) Intelligent City, 33th Carleton University Industrial design Seminar Series.

citizen-centric"[33] Indeed, potentially modern technology can tailor products to a specific customer or a group of customers, not making a common or universal world of services, but instead – creating services in a very targeted and user-centric way.[34] The main issue behind this approach is to find a balance, to create an optimal business model and recourses to meet the needs of diverse users and make services truly personalized, keeping a possibility to make a profitable business at the same time.

---

[33] California Institute for Smart Communities (2001) Smart Communities Guide Book. Available online: http://www.smartcommunities.org/guidebook.html (Last retrieved 04/08/2012)
[34] Gibson, D.V., G. Kozmetsky, R.W. Smilor, (1992) *"The Technopolis Phenomenon: Smart Cities, Fast Systems, Global Networks"*. Boston: Rowman and Littlefield Publishers,

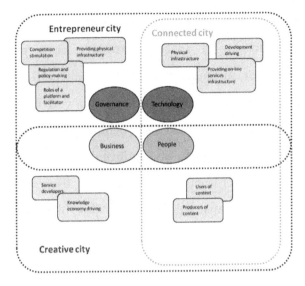

Smart Cities classification (Sashinskaya, M.)

Basic components of a Smart City

Depending on the approach of defining a smart city, we can distinguish several components or basic characteristics of it. Again, every author is explaining this set of components in his or her own way. Some of them emphasize a digital component as the most important[35], others put forward a human factor as the primary component of a smart city and the main driving force of its development.[36] Governmental,

---

[35] Landry, C (2008) The Creative City: A toolkit for urban innovators, London: Earthscan.
[36] Florida, R. (2002) *The Rise of the Creative Class: And How It's Transforming Work, Leisure, Community and Everyday life.* New

economical and environmental components are also frequently occurring parts in the list.

Nevertheless, to distinguish smart city's basic components and to structure them, we should say that some authors refer that a smart city basically consists of two layers: a real-world infrastructure and online services. [37] Komninos in his investigation of intelligent cities also proposes to separate two levels of such an urban space: *"the real level"* which refers to current technological development and people's knowledge and *"the virtual level"*, which basically means the capacity or the potential of the same people to manage knowledge and technology in the future. [38] The other group of authors agrees with Komninos, comparing systems of industrial cities with skeletons while postindustrial cities develop a nervous system with a brain as the coordination center, *"which enables them to behave in intelligently coordinated ways"*. [39]

York: Basic Books. Available at:
http://www.washingtonmonthly.com/features/2001/0205.florida.html
(Last retrieved 05/08/2012)

[37] Pentikousis, K. (2011) "Network Infrastructure at the Crossroads the Emergence of Smart Sities", Conference Publication on Intelligence in Next Generation Networks (ICIN), 15th International Conference, Berlin, 4-7 Oct. 2011.

[38] Komninos, N. (2002) *Intelligent Cities*. London: Spon Press.

[39] Harrison, C. & B. Eckman, R. Hamilton (2010) Foundations for Smarter Cities. *IBM Journal of Research and Development*, 54(4).

Anyhow, in our opinion, the most complete and concrete number of characteristics was established by researchers, working on Ranking of European medium-sized smart cities. [40]

SMART ECONOMY (Competitiveness)	SMART PEOPLE (Social and Human Capital)
• Innovative spirit • Entrepreneurship • Economic image & trademarks • Productivity • Flexibility of labour market • International embeddedness • Ability to transform	• Level of qualification • Affinity to life long learning • Social and ethnic plurality • Flexibility • Creativity • Cosmopolitanism/Open-mindedness • Participation in public life
SMART GOVERNANCE (Participation)	SMART MOBILITY (Transport and ICT)
• Participation in decision-making • Public and social services • Transparent governance • Political strategies & perspectives	• Local accessibility • (Inter-)national accessibility • Availability of ICT-infrastructure • Sustainable, innovative and safe transport systems
SMART ENVIRONMENT (Natural resources)	SMART LIVING (Quality of life)
• Attractivity of natural conditions • Pollution • Environmental protection • Sustainable resource management	• Cultural facilities • Health conditions • Individual safety • Housing quality • Education facilities • Touristic attractivity • Social cohesion

Smart cities: Ranking of European medium-sized cities. Characteristics and factors of Smart City *Giffinger, R. & C. Fertner, Kramar, H. Kalasek, R. Pichler-Milanovic, E.Meijers (2007) Smart Cities: Ranking of European Medium-Sized Cities, Research Report, Vienna University of Technology.*

---

[40] Giffinger, R. & C. Fertner, Kramar, H. Kalasek, R. Pichler-Milanovic, E.Meijers (2007) Smart Cities: Ranking of European Medium-Sized Cities, Research Report, Vienna University of Technology, Available online: http://www.smart-cities.eu/download/smart_cities_final_report.pdf (Last retrieved 22/08/2012)

The researchers conditionally have divided a potential "smartness" of a city into six categories[41]:

- Smart Economy
- Smart People
- Smart Governance
- Smart Mobility
- Smart Environment
- Smart Living

According to the methodology of the report, *"Smart Economy"* covers such elements as economic competitiveness and innovation, entrepreneurship productivity, flexibility of the labor market and inclusion and integration of a city in the national and world economics. In its turn, the *"Smart People"* component can be categorized by the level of education of the citizens as well as by the quality of social interactions and the openness and flexibility to the nearest neighbors and the whole world (cosmopolitanism ideology). *"Smart Governance"*

---

[41] Giffinger, R. & C. Fertner, Kramar, H. Kalasek, R. Pichler-Milanovic, E.Meijers (2007) Smart Cities: Ranking of European Medium-Sized Cities, Research Report, Vienna University of Technology, Available online: http://www.smart-cities.eu/download/smart_cities_final_report.pdf (Last retrieved 22/08/2012)

includes issues of transparency, active citizens' participation in political decision-making, developing public services for citizens and "smart" functioning of local administrations.

"Smart Mobility" is the next component, distinguished by the researchers from the ranking project. According to the report, local and international accessibility of an urban area as well as sustainable and innovative transport systems are important aspects for a smart city. Among other indicators, the researchers put in their methodology such indicators of "Smart Mobility" as public transport networks per inhabitant, local population satisfaction with access to public transport, indicators of usage of economical cars and non-motorized individual traffic systems. Furthermore, at the same issue of intelligent mobility, the authors distinguish the availability of information and communication technologies (ICT) and its infrastructural role in modern and sustainable transport systems. In this methodological framework the availability of computers in households and Broadband internet access in households are becoming important indexes of ICT infrastructure for a "Smart Mobility".

The next category – *"Smart Environment"* is seen by researchers as care of local communities about sustainable natural conditions, pollution reduction, natural resource management and all the issues of the environmental protection in general.

As a final point of the theory, a *"Smart Living"* component covers all the aspects of the quality of life in terms of cultural services, health issues, safety matters, housing affordability, education facilities, tourism potential, etc.

The authors of the research due to these categories have defined a Smart City as a city, which successfully operates in this entire six characteristics framework or any "smart" combination of it.

The other system of Smart City components is developed by the group of the US researchers, who also distinguish three major areas in which co-called Smart City can operate. Basically, the authors divided these components into tree big groups of factors[42]:

- Technology factors
- Institutional factors

---

[42] Nam T. & T. A. Pardo (2011) *"Conceptualizing Smart City with Dimensions of Technology, People, and Institutions",* The Proceedings of the 12th Annual International Conference on Digital Government Research, Center for Technology in Government University at Albany, State University of New York, U.S. Available online: http://www.ctg.albany.edu/publications/journals/dgo_2011_smartcity/dgo_2011_smartcity.pdf (Last retrieved 10/11/2012)

- Human factors

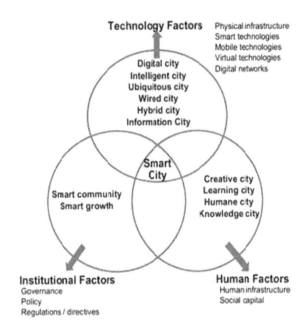

Fundamental components of Smart City [43]

According to the theory, *"Technology factors"* covers all the physical and infrastructural components as digital

---

[43] Nam T. & T. A. Pardo (2011) *"Conceptualizing Smart City with Dimensions of Technology, People, and Institutions"*, The Proceedings of the 12th Annual International Conference on Digital Government Research, Center for Technology in Government University at Albany, State University of New York, U.S. Available online: http://www.ctg.albany.edu/publications/journals/dgo_2011_smartcity/dgo_2011_smartcity.pdf (Last retrieved 10/11/2012)

networks and sustainable technological communications. The next group of smart city components is *"Human factors"*, which covers the human capital of an intelligent urban space. Finally, the third group of factors – *"Institutional factors"* refers to "Smart Governance" and issues of policy-making and law regulations development.

Finally, we would like to emphasize that even though both presented systems of smart city's basic components (the European and the US one) give different frameworks for components classification, we clearly can find a similar idea: a smart city never consists of pure ICT infrastructure or digital number of components. There are always at least two layers: a "real" or "tangible" one with all the infrastructural matters and a "virtual" or "intangible" one, which covers everything from human and policy factors to a number of modern digital services a city has. Therefore, human and community factors as well as a governmental inclusion are important for the functioning of a smart city. As a result, we can conclude that essentially there are three main blocks of components of a smart city: *Technology, People and Government.*

City (Government) as a platform

We believe that to create a holistic view of the smart city concept, we need to put more elements in our system. Except giving definitions for the smart city concept and distinguishing all of its basic components, there is a need to touch upon the idea of *"platformatization"* [44] [45] of a city. In fact, some authors describe the governmental component of a smart city, which we already considered above, in more details. In other words, they describe a city as a platform.

The "vending machine" term[46], is an illustration for the "platformatization" of the urban space idea. The concept is rather logical: when a citizen pays his taxes, he expects some services in return, and these services should clearly be provided in the place and in the time the citizen needs it. According to this idea, a government not necessarily needs to

---

[44] Walravens, N. (2011)"The City as a Platform: A Case-based Exploration of Mobile Service Platform Types in the Context of the City", Materials of the 3rd International Workshop on Business Models for Mobile Platforms (BMMP), ICIN Conference, Berlin. Available online: http://ieeexplore.ieee.org/xpls/abs_all.jsp?arnumber=6081090&tag=1 (Last retrieved 06/05/2012)

[45] [45] O'Reilly, T. (2010) Government as a Platform, Lathrop, D. & L. Ruma (eds) *Open Government*, O'Reilly Media, p.11-44

produce "smart values" by itself, but rather be a comfortable platform, working as a facilitator between private sector and citizens. In other words, a government should not create millions of apps, but needs to be a useful and stable working platform, encouraging businesses to create these apps and citizens to actively use them.

A platform can also be seen as a peculiar marketplace where citizens by themselves can exchange experiences and services. First of all, it allows people to innovate: instead of guessing what citizens need and how to meet these needs, a government can just ask people to designate their focus of interest and give the chance to a local business to propose some sustainable solutions. Secondly, it works the other way around: when a business has new services and products for more comfortable urban life to offer, a government can encourage citizens to consider consuming it. In modern understanding a government, which wants to be "smart" and open, should perform as a "mechanism for collective action"[47]. This classical in its core concept basically means that due to the right functioning of a government, citizens can interact with authorities and with each other more productively, solving their problems faster and better, making

---

[47] O'Reilly, T. (2010) Government as a Platform, Lathrop, D. & L. Ruma (eds) *Open Government*, O'Reilly Media, p.11-44

their individual and common society life more comfortable.

In terms of technological contribution, co-called "Government 2.0", [48] is not a new government, but a kind of advanced system which helps to enhance the access to governmental services to all the stakeholders through the mutual participation and use of technology. In fact, new interactive Internet tools are designed to allow citizens to participate directly in the deliberations around and drafting of government policies. [49] One of the tools of such an updated government can become the idea of "Open Data", which we will consider in more details in one of the next Chapters.

Summary and Conclusions

As we have seen during our Smart City concept investigation, most of the authors agree in general: ICTs are the core of a modern city which has its aim to be called as an

---

[48] Deloitte Consulting and Deloitte & Touche (2000) At the Dawn of e-GOVERNMENT: The Citizen as Customer. available online: http://www.egov.vic.gov.au/pdfs/e-government.pdf (Last retrieved 10/11/2012)

[49] Maura Reynolds (2009) "Open government or 'Transparency Theater?", NBS NEWS. Available online: http://www.msnbc.msn.com/id/32128642/ns/politics-cq_politics/#.UJ6dz-QsArU (Last retrieved 9/11/2012)

"intelligent" or "smart". Nevertheless, a human component, reflected in the activity and creativity of citizens and policy as well as the entrepreneurship component are important factors for defining a smart city. Thus the triangle of *"Technology-People-Government"* is becoming a strong basis for a modern intelligent city.

With the help of technology it is feasible to improve significantly everyday life of ordinary citizens through providing them with new services. In return, citizens can have a creative contribution in this process. Knowledge based businesses can definitely benefit from this smart environment by finding inspiration in an intelligent ecosystem and also giving some smart solutions to inhabitants. And finally, it is exactly a smart government which can support innovative businesses by creating proper policy-making solutions and a government which facilitates the relations between itself, businesses and its inhabitants.

A prosperous smart city project can be built with a "top down" or vice versa with a "bottom up" approach, but it goes without saying that an active involvement of every sector of the ecosystem is crucial. On the one hand, the modern urban reality is hardly imaginable without the impact of technologies, but on the other hand, devices and sensors can't replace human participation, because in the end of the day a city is about people and for people. Thus, two layers of a smart city are equally important: a real-world infrastructure and online services. Therefore, the support of the government and policy makers for smart governance is a fundamental condition for designing and implementing all kind of smart initiatives.

Chapter 2: Smart Mobility in the Context of Urban Mobility

Classical Urban Mobility

According to the United Nations report, around 50% of the world's population lives in cities and this global trend is continuing to move towards even further migration to urban areas.[50]

The global urbanization and ongoing development of big cities makes urban mobility an issue for every stakeholder, from an ordinary citizen till an administrative authority. More and more people are moving, more and more goods are being delivered in time. Because of it's definitely influence on the economy, the environment and the quality of life, urban mobility has become one of the major challenges for both the public and private sector.

Sustainable development of urban areas is no longer a theoretical topic, but rather a real issue to be practically resolved.

Numerous layers or degrees of classical urban

---

[50] United Nations (2007)The Millennium Development Goals Report. Available online:
http://www.un.org/millenniumgoals/pdf/mdg2007.pdf (Last retrieved 13/11/2012)

mobility infrastructure can be defined[51]:

- Walking
- Bicycles
- Motorcycles and Scooters
- Automobiles
- Paratransit
- Taxis
- Buses
- Bus Rapid Transit
- Trolleybuses
- Streetcars and Light Rail Transit
- Monorails
- Heavy Rail Transit (Metro)
- Commuter Rail
- Automated Guideway Transit
- Waterbourne Modes
- Parking issues as an additional issue

A typical citizen can use several types of transportation to simply move from point A to point B. For example, if a city center is a "car-free" territory, a citizen can

---

[51] Grava, S. (2003) Urban Transportation Systems: choices for communities, McGraw-Hill, Incorporated, New York, pp. 5-13

first use his personal car to get from a suburb to the city center, then park his car and use public transport or a bicycle to continue his trip. In the meantime, he can act as a pedestrian as well. Thus, we can say that urban mobility is a *multimodal phenomenon*[52] and managing this multimodality in a big city is a challenge itself.

When debates on urban mobility issues start, traditionally the problem of a growing number of private cars is popping-up as one of the first visible difficulties.[53] Indeed, very often a big number of private transport is the cause for traffic congestion in a city. Traffic jam in its turn brings economical and environmental problems to a city. Overcrowded and congested roads block the efficiency of inhabitants and, as a result, the performance, attractiveness and competitiveness of a city itself. It goes without saying that everybody wants to live in a comfortable city with a good ecology, but does it mean in a "car-free" city? According to the recent research of the French Environment and Energy Management Agency, buses and trams are more energy efficient than cars and moreover consume from 3 to 5 times

---

[52] [5] Vuchic, V. R. (1999) "Transportation for livable cities", Northwestern University, Center for Urban Policy Research, pp. 23-93

less energy per passenger.[54] It basically can be interpreted as the idea that it doesn't matter how environmentally friendly modern cars are, they still consume 3 times more energy and produce 3 times more CO_2 per passenger than public transport. Vukan R. Vuchic in his book «Transportation for Livable Cities»[55] criticizes in a way two polar ideas of better urban mobility. According to the author, using exceptionally public transport and making a city "car free" is as bad as the initiative of "transport self-service" (in other words, using personal transport by every citizen).

According to Vuchic [56], modern urban space without personal transport or so-called "car-free cities" is a utopia. The author believes that a personal car, with its unique ability to provide an excellent personal mobility, is one of the fundamental elements of the modern civilization. The availability of a personal car is a great advantage and an essential element of modern living standards. On the other hand, a city totally dependent on automobiles becomes

---

[54] The official web-site of the French Environment and Energy Management Agency. Available online: http://www2.ademe.fr/servlet/KBaseShow?sort=-1&cid=96&m=3&catid=17585

[55] [8] Vuchic, V. R. (1999) "Transportation for livable cities", Northwestern University, Center for Urban Policy Research, pp. 23-93

dysfunctional, ineffective and completely uncomfortable for to live in. As a contrary point of view to both of these theories, Vuchic opposes the idea of a city, which possesses a balanced transport system with all the types of transportation. Car-sharing can be an alternative for both approaches – it's still private transport, but also public in a way. Car-sharing is a rental model where people rent cars for a short period of time. It's a useful service for those people who only occasionally make use of a car and for those who would like to rent a different type of vehicle on different occasions. Car-sharing schemes can be also attractive for city authorities in helping resolve issues of traffic congestion, air pollution and parking availability.

Therefore, if we assume that all types of urban mobility should coexist harmoniously under the tough conditions of ever-increasing city population, the mobility should find a way to become "smarter", more efficient and well-organized. To preserve and extend public infrastructure – is one of the biggest challenges for urban mobility. We strongly believe that modern ICT as a virtual level of city's infrastructure to a certain extent can resolve urgent urban mobility issues.

"Smart" Urban Mobility

Going back to our previous thoughts on the "Basic components of a Smart City", we can distinguish "Smart Mobility" as one of the essential components.

According to the researchers, from the Vienna University of Technology[57] "Smart Mobility" is the combination of transport and ICT and can be measured by several parameters:

- sustainable, innovative and safe transport systems
- local accessibility
- national and international accessibility of a city
- accessibility of public transport networks per city inhabitant
- local population satisfaction with access to public transport
- usage of economical cars and non-motorized individual traffic systems
- availability of transport ICT infrastructure

The availability of information and communication

technologies (ICT) and its infrastructural role in modern and sustainable transport systems is one of the key concerns of the researchers[58]. In this methodological framework the availability of computers and broadband Internet access in households are becoming important indexes of ICT infrastructure for a "Smart Mobility". Therefore, we can look at a city as at the "system of systems", where two layers of urban mobility co-exist parallel and are equally important: a real infrastructural layer and a virtual or ICT-based one. As a result, an effective and smart mobility in a city can be achieved if both layers perform well.

What can be understood under the term of "Smart Mobility"? The trend is really broad and can cover all ranges of modern smart city solutions, from electric car and green public transportation concepts to so-called "networking mobility" and the role of social networks in the development of a city.[59] Equally interesting to consider a number of modern GPS (*Global Positioning System*) and navigation gadgets with or without augmented reality functions, where the user

---

[58] Giffinger, R. & C. Fertner, Kramar, H. Kalasek, R. Pichler-Milanovic, E.Meijers (2007) *Smart Cities: Ranking of European Medium-Sized Cities, Research Report, Vienna University of Technology*, Available online: http://www.smart-cities.eu/download/smart_cities_final_report.pdf (Last retrieved 22/08/2012)

[59] Vuchic, V. R. (1999) "Transportation for livable cities", Northwestern University, Center for Urban Policy Research, pp. 23-93

can switch between a regular topographic map and a "two-dimensional" or even "3D" navigation, getting a realistic perception of a route.[60] These types of applications via ICT literally combine and mix two layers of urban infrastructure: the real and the virtual one. This convergence of classical cartography, new media and ICT not only brings practical benefits for city navigation, but also creates new urban esthetics and extends citizens' personal experience.

The last, but not the least factor, which makes urban mobility "smarter", is the cost-efficiency. For a city it's crucial indeed to be not only modern, comfortable and attractive for living, but also economically efficient. In the end it's all about tax-payers, who expect a comfortable life style in the area.

According to resent case studies reports[61], sustainable or "smart" mobility is a sum of three essential components:

• **social inclusion** (when all the residents regardless of social status, age, gender, physical conditions are able to be mobile in the city)

---

[60] Foth, M. (Ed.) (2009). "Navigation Becomes Travel Scouting: The Augmented Spaces of Car Navigation Systems", *Handbook of Research on Urban Informatics: The Practice and Promise of the Real-Time City*. Hershey, PA, pp. 230-241
[61] City of Stuttgart (2009) *Agenda 21 for Urban Mobility*, pp. 6-40.

- **friendly environment** (reducing air and noise pollution and minimizing traffic flows through integrated urban and traffic planning)
- **economy promotion** (better logistics, improving the efficiency of transit companies).

Role of data in the "Smart Mobility" concept

Every day a modern city generates and collects a lot of data. All this information can be deliberately collected and stored by special public services (e.g. city statistics agencies) manually or with the help of technology (smart grids and sensors). Data can also be collected through the contribution of ordinary citizens (crowdsoursing and social media platforms), via technology (traffic cameras and sensors) or manually (again, citizens' monitoring). All this amount of data can become a prominent driving force in increasing urban mobility through ICT technologies. Hence, providing transport information can actively assist people in changing their daily movement actions. [62]

For example, Fioretti in his report indicates that many

---

[62] Thomas, S. (2009) Slim City, materials of the World Economic Forum, slide 14 Available online: http://www.driversofchange.com/slimcity/downloads/urban_mobility_l ow_res.pdf (Last retrieved 11/11/2012)

people are aware about possible reduction of air pollution through changing of their habits – using public transport instead of private cars. However, a big number of cities' inhabitants still prefer cars, because, according to the author, public transportation is an unpredictable issue and it's often more reliable for citizens to use a private car. This is why re-use of trustworthy and real-time geolocation data can be a solution for a city: *"Having correct, real time information about how much time and money it will take to go somewhere with public buses, taxis and trains or how much time one should spend waiting at some bus stop is a big, very important support and stimulus to use public transportation more".* [63]

Many cities now have started to provide data on official transport companies' websites. Very often citizens can also find on these web recourses interactive maps and some journey-planners, which helps to calculate travel time and cost per every single city trip. Up-dates about planned roadworks or spontaneous events as, for example, public transport strikes can also be available on-line. [64] Geolocation

---

[63] Fioretti, M. (2011)" Open Data: Emerging trends, issues and best practices", *Laboratory of Economics and Management of Scuola Superiore Sant'Anna,* Pisa, pp. 7-18.

[64] Bührmann, S. & F. Wefering, S. Rupprecht (2011) Guidlines: Developing and implementing a sustainable urban mobility plan, Munich, pp. 6-15. Available online: http://www.mobilityweek.eu/fileadmin/files/docs/SUMP_guidelines_web0.pdf (Last retrieved 13/11/2012)

data are especially important when it creates an added social and economic value in combination with any other public sector information. In some cases, these data are available only for non-commercial or personal use, in others – it's fully open and interoperable data, which is allowed to be re-used by web-developers to create new types of desktop and mobile applications for city mobility. In one of the next Chapters we will look at the "open data" and open governmental data phenomenon in more details.

Another remarkable ICT trend and a potential tool for "smart mobility" is *crowdsourcing* or "soft info"[65], when a large number of city volunteers wish and ready to contribute in any public system improving.[66] A participatory way of contributing to the wealth and quality of life can be promoted via urban crowdsourcing. According to the group of MIT researchers[67], the key characteristics of a modern city is the circulation of information in a real-time principle. Basically, social media and crowdsoursing platforms can support this

---

[65] Koetsier, J. (2012) An operating system for cities: How IBM plans to make your city smarter, VentureBeat. Available online: http://venturebeat.com/2012/06/29/ibm-city-operating-system/ (Last retrieved 13/11/2012)

[66] Fioretti, M. (2011)" Open Data: Emerging trends, issues and best practices", *Laboratory of Economics and Management of Scuola Superiore Sant'Anna,* Pisa, pp. 7-18.

[67] Foth, M. (Ed.) (2009). "WikiCity: Real-time location-sensitive tools for the city", *Handbook of Research on Urban Informatics: The Practice and Promise of the Real-Time City.* Hershey, PA, p. 397

idea as long as a critical mass of users is reporting and exchanging their data. On the other hand, the authors doubt if the information provided by an open community source can be reliable.[68] According to the researchers, this issue can be resolved with the implementation of a system of "publicity recognized certificates", which makes a source trustworthy and useful.

Open city data, crowdsoursing data and data provided by private and state transport companies can be available in real time mode on citizens' devices such as PC, tablets and smartphones. Combinations of different sources of information make data more reliable and linked datasets relations create new informational value. Ideally, apps and interconnected devices can be integrated in everyday city life in a way people don't recognize their presence anymore.[69]

[68.] Foth, M. (Ed.) (2009). "WikiCity: Real-time location-sensitive tools for the city", *Handbook of Research on Urban Informatics: The Practice and Promise of the Real-Time City*. Hershey, PA, p. 392

An overview of the EU initiatives on Smart Mobility

According to the EU statistics, over 60% of the Union population lives in urban areas and at the same time 75% of all private transport usage is driving inside cities.[70] Preferably, European cities should remain places comfortable for living, working and going for leisure. Thus, an efficient, safe and more environmentally friendly urban mobility is an essential guarantee for a high quality of life.

In the beginning of the 21st century many developed territories in the EU were motivated to enhance their mobility and at the same time to reduce road congestion, traffic, air pollution, insecurity and accidents in European cities. Thus, a few documents have been launched to support these initiatives at the EU regulation level.

In September 2007 the European Commission launched the Green Paper on smart mobility, calling "Towards a new culture for urban mobility". The aim of the paper was to set up a new EU agenda for urban mobility and open a round of debates on the urban priorities such as

---

[70] EUROPEAN COMMISSION (2008) *Citizens summary on the Green Paper "Towards a new culture for urban mobility",* Available online: http://ec.europa.eu/transport/themes/urban/urban_mobility/green_paper/doc/2008_citizen_summary.pdf (Last retrieved 13/11/2012)

greener cities, smarter urban transport, accessibility and security of public transport for the EU citizens. [71]

Later on, in September 2009, the European Commission adopted the Action Plan on urban mobility.[72] The paper proposes twenty measures for planning and managing urban transport and making city travelling easier. These measures cover the necessity of sharing information between Member States in order to find successful solutions. The measures also establish some additional work with stakeholders in order to defend the rights of public transport users (e.g. providing better information on public transport services in the EU cities). Moreover, the paper is aimed to improve data collection for better policy making. Even though the responsibility for transport in urban areas is mainly a Member States' business, the EU sees the ability to assist the national authorities in developing standard solutions

---

[71] EUROPEAN COMMISSION. COM(2007) 551 final. GREEN PAPER Towards a new culture for urban mobility. 25.9.2007. Available online: http://eur-lex.europa.eu/LexUriServ/LexUriServ.do?uri=COM:2007:0551:FIN:EN:PDF (Last retrieved 11/11/2012)

[72] EUROPEAN COMMISSION. COM(2009) 490 final. COMMUNICATION FROM THE COMMISSION TO THE EUROPEAN PARLIAMENT, THE COUNCIL, THE EUROPEAN ECONOMIC AND SOCIAL COMMITTEE AND THE COMMITTEE OF THE REGIONS Action Plan on Urban Mobility, 30.9.2009. Available online: http://eur-lex.europa.eu/LexUriServ/LexUriServ.do?uri=COM:2009:0490:FIN:EN:PDF (Last retrieved 11/11/2012)

and making the EU transport market more integrated. Thus, with the Action Plan on urban mobility the European Commission plans to encourage and help local, regional and national authorities in achieving their goals for a sustainable urban mobility.

The Digital Agenda for Europe, a flagship initiative of the EU which was launched in August 2010 and aimed to develop a digital single market in the territory of the European Union, is also mentioning a need of developing ITS (intelligent transport systems) for efficient transport and better mobility. [73] The paper supports the exploitation of real-time traffic data, travel information and active usage of traffic management systems to resolve traffic congestion issues and at the same time support green mobility and enhance security. According to the paper, the Commission is leading the support of the EU cross-border services, providing passengers with *"journey planning tools (including connections to other trains and modes, support for reservation, payment and luggage tracing)*

---

[73] EUROPEAN COMMISSION. COM (2010) 245 final. Communication from the Commission to the European Parliament, the Council, the European Economic and Social Committee and the Committee of the Regions, a Digital Agenda for Europe. 19.5.2010. Available online: http://eur-lex.europa.eu/LexUriServ/LexUriServ.do?uri=COM:2010:0245:FIN:EN:PDF (Last retrieved 15/09/2012)

as well as real time updates". [74]

In other words, the EU authorities are establishing legal and ideological frameworks to support and coordinate smart urban mobility initiatives in the EU, by setting general conditions and promoting it across the borders amongst the Member States.

Summary and Conclusions

The global urbanization processes make cities bigger and as a result a the multimodal urban mobility is becoming an issue. The way of looking at the city as at the "system of systems" is giving a perspective to distinguish two parallel essential layers of modern urban mobility: a real infrastructural layer with roads, transport and parking facilities and a virtual one, based on ICT development. "Smart Mobility" is a crucial component of a "Smart City", as long as it affects all the stakeholders, from city inhabitants to

---

[74] EUROPEAN COMMISSION. COM (2010) 245 final. Communication from the Commission to the European Parliament, the Council, the European Economic and Social Committee and the Committee of the Regions, a Digital Agenda for Europe. 19.5.2010. Available online: http://eur-lex.europa.eu/LexUriServ/LexUriServ.do?uri=COM:2010:0245:FIN:EN:PDF (Last retrieved 15/09/2012)

the local business. Thus, if we take into consideration how much data a modern city and its citizens generate and collect every day, we can definitely assume that these data can create added social and economic value, especially if it's linked and combined with other public data resources. To follow the trends, to regulate cities' mobility and the ICT impact on mobility issues and promote the best practices across the Member States, the EU institutions are setting up legal and conceptual initiatives containing some general rules.

Chapter 3: Open Data concept in a discourse of Smart Cities

What is Open Data?

The number of countries around the globe that put the "Open Data" concept on its political and administrative agenda is increasing significantly. Most of the time, authorities implement open data strategies to increase transparency, citizen participation and government performance efficiency.[75] Big organizations like OECD (Organization for Economic Co-operation and Development)[76], and UNESCO [77] also have started to promote open access to information and knowledge. Even though in case of UNESCO it is mostly about the right to access scientific information, the main idea of *"Open access is*

---

[75] Huijboom, N. & T. Van den Broek (2011) "Open data: an international comparison of strategies", *European Journal of ePractice*, 12 (March/April 2011), pp. 4-15. Available online: http://www.epractice.eu/files/European%20Journal%20epractice%20Volume%2012_4.pdf (Last retrieved 15/08/2012)

[76] OECD (2007) "Principles and Guidelines for Access to Research Data from Public Funding" Available online: http://www.oecd.org/science/scienceandtechnologypolicy/38500813.pdf (Last retrieved 21/09/2012)

[77] Swan, A. (2012) "Policy Guidelines for the Development and Promotion of Open Access", *Published by the United Nations Educational, Scientific and Cultural Organization – UNESCO*. Available online:
http://unesdoc.unesco.org/images/0021/002158/215863e.pdf (Last retrieved 21/09/2012)

about Freedom, Flexibility and Fairness" [78] can be borrowed for all the open data types.

Although the portal with public sector information datasets was launched quite recently in 2009[79], the US federal government initiative on increasing public access to governmental information can be treated as a flagman of the initiative around the globe, On his first working day as the United States President in January 2009, Barack Obama announced that his team would start a transparent open government strategy: *" We will work together to ensure the public trust and establish a system of transparency, public participation, and collaboration. Openness will strengthen our democracy and promote efficiency and effectiveness in Government."* [80]

In this perspective, the European Union has slightly longer history of dealing with open data. The first attempts

---

[78] Swan, A. (2012) "Policy Guidelines for the Development and Promotion of Open Access", *Published by the United Nations Educational, Scientific and Cultural Organization – UNESCO*, pp. 6-12. Available online:
http://unesdoc.unesco.org/images/0021/002158/215863e.pdf (Last retrieved 21/09/2012)
[79] The US Federal Government open data web portal: http://www.data.gov/ (Last retrieved 15/10/2012)
[80] Obama, B. (2009) "Memorandum for the Heads of Executive Departments and Agencies: Transparency and Open Government". Available online:
http://www.whitehouse.gov/the_press_office/TransparencyandOpenGovernment
(Last retrieved 29/09/2012)

have been made in 2003 with launching pan-European Directive on public sector information re-use or shortly - PSI-Directive. [81] The Commissioner responsible for the Digital Agenda implementation, Neelie Kroes accentuated the idea that nowadays data is a kind of new fuel: *"Data is new oil for a digital era"*.[82] Thus, by opening up governmental data it is possible to provide stakeholders with an amount of new economical, political and social values, needed to the EU modern society. Nowadays, the website of the European Union [83] is one of the biggest web recourses in the world. It contains and at the same time gives access to more than 6 million pages of all types of information and legislative acts of the EU. [84] Thus, many essential data already exist in digital format, and still governments constantly continue to generate new amounts of data. [85] [86] Nevertheless, different authorities

---

[81] EUROPEAN PARLIAMENT & COUNCIL (2003) Directive 2003/98/EC of the European Parliament and the Council of 17 November 2003, on the re-use of public sector information.
[82] Kroes, N. (2012) Speech on ePSI conference in Rotterdam March 2012. Available online:
http://www.youtube.com/watch?v=9Jq4Qy1UeAE (Last retrieved 03/11/2012)
[83] The official website of the European Union. Available online: http://europa.eu/ (Last retrieved 15/10/2012)
[84] Curtin, D.& A. Meijer (2006) "Does Transparency Strengthen Legitimacy? A Critical Analysis of European Union Policy Documents", *Information Polity,* 11(2006), pp. 109-122.
[85] Uhlir, P.F. (2009) "The Socioeconomic Effects of Public Sector Information on Digital Networks: Toward a Better Understanding of Different Access and Reuse Policies: Workshop Summary", *US National Committee CODATA, in cooperation with OECD,* pp. 25-39.

in different countries have their special views, motivations and official positions whether they make their PSI available or not. Even if some data are available, it's up to a national authority which terms and conditions implement to information be reused: from completely open access to limited or charged access.[87]

Anyhow, while the amount of any kinds of digital information, from mapping, social statistics and weather forecasting to private companies monitoring, is growing, public bodies have to find solutions how to maintain all this structured and unstructured data at least for their own internal needs and for the needs of society and business as well. [88] [89]

A widespread and commonly accepted argument for

---

[86] Fioretti, M. (2011)" Open Data: Emerging trends, issues and best practices", *Laboratory of Economics and Management of Scuola Superiore Sant'Anna,* Pisa, pp. 3-7.

[87] Uhlir, P.F. (2009) "The Socioeconomic Effects of Public Sector Information on Digital Networks: Toward a Better Understanding of Different Access and Reuse Policies: Workshop Summary", *US National Committee CODATA, in cooperation with OECD,* pp. 9-24.

[88] Fioretti, M. (2011)" Open Data: Emerging trends, issues and best practices", *Laboratory of Economics and Management of Scuola Superiore Sant'Anna,* Pisa, pp. 5-15.

[89] Directorate General for the Information Society (2000) Commercial Exploitation of Europe's Public Sector Information: Final Report. Available online: http://ec.europa.eu/information_society/policy/psi/docs/pdfs/pira_study/commercial_final_report.pdf (Last retrieved 05/07/2012)

implementing open data strategies is that opening-up of governmental data in a reusable format can strengthen citizen engagement and force businesses to innovate. However, the open data phenomenon is relatively new and evidence of an expected positive impact still needs to be proven in more detail. Moreover, the idea of opening-up and re-using public sector information is not a neutral one. Some researchers are biased, arguing that radical openness may result in unpleasant accidents and an even further lack of trust to the government. [90] [91] Nevertheless, in this paper we are not going to evaluate positive or negative impact of re-using public sector information in a deep way, as we believe it's the topic of a separate academic research. Instead, we would like to look at the phenomenon in a nutshell, to give some definitions, characteristics, types and legal basis of open data initiatives with mandatory providing the research with some essential critics on the topic.

---

[90] Fioretti, M. (2011)" Open Data: Emerging trends, issues and best practices", *Laboratory of Economics and Management of Scuola Superiore Sant'Anna,* Pisa, pp. 3-27.
[91] Dutra, M. (2011) Dangers of Open Government Data, *The Networked Society Blog.* Retrieved from: http://thenetworkedsociety.blogspot.be/2011/03/dangers-of-open-government-data.html

Giving definitions to Open Data

For some reasons the amount of academic literature on open data topic is quite limited. Probably it refers to relative novelty of the concept. Giving many diverse definitions of this practice is therefore almost unfeasible at this moment. Thus, we will refer to descriptions which can be found in works of independent researchers and public open data activists. First of all, it's interesting to look at the definition which Open Knowledge Foundation[92]- the main organization advocating for opening-up governmental data around the globe - gives:

"Open data – data which is able to be used for any purpose;

Public Sector Information (PSI) – information collected or controlled by the public sector;

Open Government Data – open data produced by the government. This is generally accepted to be data gathered during the course of business as usual activities which do not identify individuals or breach commercial sensitivity. Open government data is a subset of

---

[92] The official website of the Open Knowledge Foundation. Available online: http://okfn.org/ (Last retrieved 01/10/2012)

Public Sector Information, which is broader in scope".[93]

We strongly believe that the meaning of "Public Sector Information" (PSI) shouldn't be mixed up with the meaning of "open data". They are not necessarily synonyms in cases when PSI is stored by government and not opened up for the other stakeholders as citizens, commercial and non-commercial organizations. Anyhow, PSI and open data definitions can overlap and even be identical in situations where public sector information is under the open access. For example, if government collects and stores some transport or traffic congestions data, these information is PSI, because it's *"information collected or controlled by the public sector"* and obviously it's done on taxpayers' money. These information can become an "open data" only when it is announced, published and *"able to be used for any purpose"*. Any non-governmental entity can also make its private information open for a public and make it "open data". It basically means, that "open data" is not necessarily governmental data either. Thus, these two types of information (PSI and open data) are not automatically the same things, even though in some cases we can talk about PSI as a form of open data.

---

[93] Open Knowledge Foundation (2012) Open Data Handbook. Available online: http://opendatahandbook.org/en/glossary.html#term-public-sector-information (Last retrieved 01/10/2012)

In the report for the European Commission on the topic of commercial exploitation of PSI, Public Sector Information is defined as *"...information created, collected, developed and disseminated by the public sector"* [94]

The other Commission definition on open public data is following: *"Public data is all the information that public bodies in the European Union produce, collect or pay for. This could include geographical data, statistics, meteorological data, data from publicly funded research projects, and digitised books from libraries"*. [95]

The author of the open data best practices research, Marco Fioretti, also identifies PSI as *"data that is of public interest, that belongs to the whole community, data that every citizen is surely entitled to know and use"*. [96]

In other words, collecting all this definitions and extracting the most important ideas out of it, we can define open data and open PSI as **produced, collected and stored**

---

[94] Directorate General for the Information Society (2000) Commercial Exploitation of Europe's Public Sector Information: Final Report, pp. 8-14. Available online: http://ec.europa.eu/information_society/policy/psi/docs/pdfs/pira_study/commercial_final_report.pdf (Last retrieved 05/07/2012)
[95] The official website of the European Union (2012) Digital Agenda: Commission's Open Data Strategy, Questions & answers. Available online: http://europa.eu/rapid/press-release_MEMO-11-891_en.htm?locale=en (Last retrieved 13/08/2012)
[96] Fioretti, M. (2011)" Open Data: Emerging trends, issues and best practices", *Laboratory of Economics and Management of Scuola Superiore Sant'Anna,* Pisa, pp. 3-27

by governmental and public service bodies information, which are expected to become freely available on-line for other stakeholders as citizens, public organizations and business structures. Furthermore it's important to mention that data should be collected, stored and presented in a digital form, even if initially it was generated in a traditional paper way. From the moment datasets have been digitalized, they can be disseminated and new data can be built on its basis. [97]

Open Data classification

Fioretti[98] gives some typology of open data, which we find the most comprehensive and clear classification at the moment. By adding some European Commission descriptions and clarifications[99], we can present fairly

---

[97] Murray-Rust, P. (2012) BioIT 2009 – What is data? *Personal blog on open knowledge.* Available online:
http://blogs.ch.cam.ac.uk/pmr/2009/04/29/bioit-2009-what-is-data-1/
(Last retrieved 04/11/2012)

[98] Fioretti, M. (2011)" Open Data: Emerging trends, issues and best practices", *Laboratory of Economics and Management of Scuola Superiore Sant'Anna,* Pisa, pp. 3-27

[99] Directorate General for the Information Society (2000) Commercial Exploitation of Europe's Public Sector Information: Final Report, pp. 8-14. Available online:
http://ec.europa.eu/information_society/policy/psi/docs/pdfs/pira_study/commercial_final_report.pdf (Last retrieved 05/07/2012)

complete, in our opinion, the typology of open data.

Types of Open data with examples:

- Geographical and Local transportation data (maps, land exploitation, cadastre information, addresses, public transport schedules and real-time performance, street cameras images, traffic data etc.)

- Demographic data (age and sex information about city inhabitants, birth and death statistics etc.)

- Election data (activity of the local administration members, their everyday work statistics and voting preferences on each relevant city topic, law proposals statuses etc.)

- Budgets and taxes data (salaries of public authorities, local budget lines spending)

- Security and legal data (crime statistics, police performances, law enforcement)

- Local activities data (location and contact information of the public and private services)

- Real Estate data (household locations, apartment's prices, time traveling from one household to another or to a public service body etc.)

- Energy and water production and consumption data (energy and water consumption data from citizens, public bodies and industry)

- Environmental data and pollution measurements (air, water and land pollution rates, possible harmful emissions from industrial sector or public and private transport)

- Waste and water management data (garbage collection schedules for each neighborhood, amount of water wasting, how much money spent on it etc.)

- Health-related data (hospital performances, spread of infections)

- Education data (school locations and costs, student grades performances in every school, sex and average age of students, available resources as libraries and gyms etc.)

- Agricultural and fisheries data (crop fields areas, the number of fish caught per year etc.)

• Scientific data (research of the universities, publicly-funded research institutes, patents information etc.).

• Cultural data (materials of museums, art galleries, exhibitions, festivals, library resources etc.)

Apparently, the value of any type of PSI is increasing exponentially when it can be combined and linked with other data. For example, a family can make a decision to move to another city. Geographical and public transport data can be combined with real estate data and security and crime statistics to choose a better neighborhood for living. Energy and water consumption data combined with health and education data can help in planning the family budget. And finally, cultural and election data can give them an idea what the community looks like, which values and priorities are shared by neighbors and local administration. This complex of open data can give to a family, which decided to live in a new city, a holistic picture of a new living place and make possible expectations more or less objective from the very beginning.

Nevertheless, we believe that the list of open data types can be longer and probably will expand due to new open datasets.

What is real "openness"?

To call data "open" we should distinguish a number of characteristics, which can make particular information open. Peter Murray-Rust, a chemist from Cambridge Center of Molecular informatics, who is currently working on issues of general "openness" of information, presents some universal conditions for open data.[100]

First of all, according to the scientist, the fundamental rule of any open information is its possibility to be re-used because any barrier to this process can damage a semantic value of data. Among other conditions of "openness", Peter Murray-Rust also argues to abilities of data to be redistributed, attributed, integrated and not to be discriminated against persons, groups and fields of endeavor including any commercial using. According to the author of the classification, all the conditions are mandatory and none of them can be optional.

The other system of "openness" evaluation is less strict and rather flexible. In 2010 the Director of the World Wide Web Consortium, Tim Bernes-Lee, proposed a "5-star

---

[100] Murray-Rust, P. (2012) BioIT 2009 – What is data? *Personal blog on open knowledge.* Available online: http://blogs.ch.cam.ac.uk/pmr/2009/04/27/bioit-in-boston-what-is-open/ (Last retrieved 04/11/2012)

system for open data". [101] This rating system is aimed to help public sector bodies to work on opening-up their data.

Number of stars	Meaning
no stars	Information is available on-line, but not available to be re-used under an open license
1 star	Information is available on-line under an open license, but understandable only for a human eye (text format)
2 stars	Information is available on-line under an open license, structured and available for machines (Excel format)
3 stars	Information is available on-line under an open license, structured and available for machines (no dependency on a particular software producer)
4 stars	Information is available on-line under an open license, structured, available for machines and has it's unique URI (Uniform Resource Identifier)

---

[101] Berners-Lee, T. (2010) Speech on "Open, Linked Data for a Global Community", *Gov 2.0 Expo 2010*. Available online: http://www.youtube.com/watch?feature=player_embedded&v=ga1aSJXCFe0 (Last retrieved 17/11/2012)

	5 stars	Information is available on-line under an open license, structured, available for machines, has it's unique URI and can be linked and interconnected to other data using network effects and creating new value

Five-star system for open data

Berners-Lee, T. (2010) Speech on "Open, Linked Data for a Global Community", Gov 2.0 Expo 2010.

The main idea of this "5-star system for open data" is to show that public data can be completely useful only if it has an ability to be linked with other data sets and create new social and economical value. Thus, **interoperability** is a crucial issue in the open data discourse. This universal characteristic allows different components of complex systems to work together. We can even compare the nature of interoperability with a common technological language. Anyway, an interoperability can be defined as "a result of mixing data and pieces of content from different sources and re-using it in unexpected ways" [102]

Going back to the Cambridge scientist Peter Murray-Rust thoughts on open data, it seems evident that some of

---

[102] EVPSI/LAPSI (2012) Web streaming of the 4th LAPSI Internal Conference and EVPSI/LAPSI Final Meeting (9th/10th July 2012). Retrieved from: http://www.lapsi-project.eu/streaming

public authorities' on-line resources, which are positioning themselves as "open", are not really that open. According to the scientist, it can be judged by several parameters:[103]

- only part of data are available

- there are limits to the amount of downloaded data

- re-use is forbidden because of copyrights to the information

- data are not marked as open (through open licenses) and thus, the possibility to use it is vague

Therefore, at this stage of open data initiatives implementations, we can talk about existing division between "complete openness" and "selective openness" approaches. Obviously "something" is always better than "nothing" and the process of opening-up and re-using of PSI has started recently. More attention to it should be given and more work should be done by public sector bodies around the globe and in the EU in particular.

---

[103] Murray-Rust, P. (2012) BioIT 2009 – What is data? *Personal blog on open knowledge.* Available online: http://blogs.ch.cam.ac.uk/pmr/2009/04/27/bioit-in-boston-what-is-open/ (Last retrieved 04/11/2012)

Governmental motivations to open-up its data

The idea behind the open data concept is quite simple. First of all, the right to knowledge is a basic principle of democracy, and if a government is ready to become transparent and innovative, all the public value data should be easily accessible for citizens (whether it's state spending reports, pollution rates or public transport data).

Moreover, citizens have already paid from their taxes for collecting and storing all this huge amount of data and now these data can and should be re-used for their benefits and even by themselves.

Some researches even emphasize that keeping data closed is much more expensive than putting it online. [104] So, if data are still being collected, what to do with all this information and how can it really make the choice of citizens wider and the governmental work more effective? In this respect the researchers of the open data phenomenon distinguish three primary motivations for a government to

---

[104] Fioretti, M. (2011)" Open Data: Emerging trends, issues and best practices", *Laboratory of Economics and Management of Scuola Superiore Sant'Anna,* Pisa, pp. 3-27

create open data strategies[105]:

- Increasing democratic control and political participation of citizens;

- Pushing law enforcement;

- Fostering services and products innovations

First of all, launching of a big amount of datasets can increase democratic control and political participation of citizens: *"Open Data transform not just the way services are delivered but, more importantly, allow citizens to control those services."* [106] Perhaps, without the Internet broad transparency would be unfeasible and much more expensive. Curtin and Meijer say that the Internet is a significant platform and at the same time a driver for transparency. [107] Basically, if the information is open and the more people can have free access to it, the

---

[105] Huijboom, N. & T. Van den Broek (2011) "Open data: an international comparison of strategies", *European Journal of ePractice*, 12 (March/April 2011), pp. 4-15. Available online: http://www.epractice.eu/files/European%20Journal%20epractice%20Volume%2012_4.pdf (Last retrieved 15/08/2012)

[106] Brown, G. (2010) Speech of the Prime Minister on Building Britain's Digital Future, London. Available online: http://webarchive.nationalarchives.gov.uk/+/number10.gov.uk/news/speeches-and-transcripts/2010/03/speech-on-building-britains-digital-future-22897 (Last retrieved 03/06/2012)

[107] Curtin, D.& A. Meijer (2006) "Does Transparency Strengthen Legitimacy? A Critical Analysis of European Union Policy Documents", *Information Polity,* 11(2006), pp. 109-122

more reasons for a government to be crystal clear by performing a public task. On the other hand, some researches argue that opening-up data is not a guarantee for a government to be transparent: *"There is no automatic cause-effect relationship between Open Data and real transparency and democracy. On the contrary, several problems may occur, if administrators and citizens don't pay close attention".* [108] Later on in this Chapter we will look through possible negative effects of open data in more detail.

Second possible reason for governments to open their data, and we believe this motive is linked with the first one (transparency), is pushing a law enforcement and involving citizens in legislation monitoring. [109]City crime statistics and budget spending can be examples of this issue. Obviously, here a government is becoming closer to citizens by opening up and sharing its significant and quite delicate information.

Finally, the third primer motive for a government to create open data strategies (and we believe this motive could

---

[108] Fioretti, M. (2011)" Open Data: Emerging trends, issues and best practices", *Laboratory of Economics and Management of Scuola Superiore Sant'Anna,* Pisa, pp. 3-27

[109] Huijboom, N. & T. Van den Broek (2011) "Open data: an international comparison of strategies", *European Journal of ePractice,* 12 (March/April 2011), pp. 4-15. Available online: http://www.epractice.eu/files/European%20Journal%20epractice%20Volume%2012_4.pdf (Last retrieved 15/08/2012)

be probably the most promising in the digital age), is fostering services and products innovations. [110] Talking about the open data phenomenon it's important to mention that the interest of local and national authorities can be stimulated not only by internal reasons of transparency and public loyalty, but also by external motives as technologies development and local business interests. Reasonable to say, the rise of the social networks and increasing role of mobile Internet in everyday life encourages businesses to the creation of new services based on the government data.

Collecting, analyzing and using data can be beneficial to non-governmental sectors. In fact, the wide range of open data sets can potentially encourage businesses to find a way to make profit out of re-using PSI and innovate in a private sector. If we go back to our attempts to explain the Smart City concept and remind the idea of "government is a platform", we will also investigate that the authors believe that the most successful platforms are open platforms because the power of open standards is cultivates innovation. The logic is simple: if it's easy for an entrepreneur to enter the market - the innovation goes natural and free, instead

---

[110] Huijboom, N. & T. Van den Broek (2011) "Open data: an international comparison of strategies", *European Journal of ePractice*, 12 (March/April 2011), pp. 4-15. Available online: http://www.epractice.eu/files/European%20Journal%20epractice%20Volume%2012_4.pdf (Last retrieved 15/08/2012)

"when barriers are high, innovation moves elsewhere". [111] Moreover, according the other group of authors, the main advantage of open data is exactly in the fact that the nature of openness works both ways: for the transparency and for the innovation, because developers very often re-use data in really unexpected and very creative ways. The Economist magazine also agrees with the idea that the potential of PSI is yet not explored till the end: "The data-centered economy is just nascent". [112]

Taking into account these tree basic motivations for a modern government, obviously, open data recourses can become a natural advantage of smart cities.[113] When we say that open data recourses are a natural advantage, we also refer to the pre-paid character of this information. The information is already collected and stored by local and pan-European authorities. It means that for this re-using no big amount of money is needed (except if there is the need to transform public sector information data into machine-

---

[111] O'Reilly, T. (2010) Government as a Platform, Lathrop, D. & L. Ruma (eds) *Open Government*, O'Reilly Media, p.11-44
[112] Group of authors (2010) Data, data, everywhere, *The Economist*, Special Report, Feb 25, 2010. Available online:
http://www.economist.com/node/15557443 (Last retrieved 04/11/2012)
[113] Pentikousis, K. (2011) "Network Infrastructure at the Crossroads the Emergence of Smart Sities", Conference Publication on Intelligence in Next Generation Networks (ICIN), 15th International Conference, Berlin, 4-7 Oct. 2011.

readable formats and putting it on special on-line portals). A city already has statistical data recourses and the recourse itself is quite natural for the territory in terms of governmental effort to get it.

Critics of Open Data concept

Many world governments nowadays have open data programs. Some of the strategies are quite successful and effective in opening-up datasets, others – not even trying to improve the level of "openness", preferring to have programs only on paper.

Fioretti is wondering: *"If openness is so good, why aren't all Public Data already open?"*[114] Indeed, the question is rational and the author is trying to find the answer, arguing to different reasons from lack of sustainable physical infrastructures and Internet connections to abridging the freedom of speech.

Among others, the author distinguishes further reasons why some governments are not very active in opening-up their data sets:

---

[114] Fioretti, M. (2011)" Open Data: Emerging trends, issues and best practices", *Laboratory of Economics and Management of Scuola Superiore Sant'Anna,* Pisa, pp. 3-27

- Lack of legal framework, legal barriers and copyright law domination

- Lack of awareness and guiding about potential benefits of PSI re-use

- Biases against security issues

- Unwillingness to publish low quality and inaccurate data

- Lack of funds to transform data into machine-readable format and/or to publish it

To be objective and make our research balanced we find it necessary to indicate and systematize possible controversial issues of open data, the reasons for governments to stop implementing open data strategies.

- First of all, a clear definition of PSI and open data is needed.

Is PSI can be all the information produced by governments and public bodies? In fact, city administrations are normally also responsible for monitoring activities of private companies. Can this still be considered as PSI in case of anonymization statistical data or should this issue be protected under the privacy law?[115] What if published data is inaccurate or not up-to-date?

Imagine a traffic management application based on this data – it can be a cause of even more congestion on certain roads.

• Not only inaccurate, but also intentionally manipulated data can be potentially published by public bodies.

As long as people trust official information and don't verify or double check it[116], the risk that data is manipulated can even decrease the trust in the government. Thus, stakeholders and users should still think critically about where data comes from and through/with which principles it was collected. [117] Some open data sets, together with proper analytics, can make people prejudged.

---

[115] Fioretti, M. (2011)" Open Data: Emerging trends, issues and best practices", *Laboratory of Economics and Management of Scuola Superiore Sant'Anna,* Pisa, pp. 13-23

[116] Dutra, M. (2011) Dangers of Open Government Data, *The Networked Society Blog*. Retrieved from: http://thenetworkedsociety.blogspot.be/2011/03/dangers-of-open-government-data.html (Last retrieved 04/11/2012)

[117] Fioretti, M. (2011)" Open Data: Emerging trends, issues and best practices", *Laboratory of Economics and Management of Scuola Superiore Sant'Anna,* Pisa, pp. 3-27

For example, it's quite delicate to open up statistics of which district in the city is the most polluted or which part of the city has the highest crime rate, because people simply can start trying to avoid these places. Again, what if the data in this case are not accurate?

- There is a common threat that some people can exploit PSI in a wrong or illegal way.

For example, opening up a map of public toilets can provoke perverts activity. In this discourse we would like to use a clear example which the Canadian open government activist David Eaves gives in his blog.[118] When a government builds a road, this road potentially can be used by both – a robber, who can run away from police through this road and for an ambulance car, which takes the road to save someone's life. Should a government reject the idea to build a new road only because it can be potentially used for illegal actions? As a result: instead of rejecting the idea of opening-up PSI, a legal framework for dealing with open data crimes should be better developed.

---

[118] Eaves, D. (2010) How Governments misunderstand the risks of Open Data, Personal Blog. Retrieved from: http://eaves.ca/2010/10/06/how-governments-misunderstand-the-risks-of-open-data/ (Last retrieved 04/11/2012)

- One more thing which should be developed in a legal frame work is the question of licensing open data.

In some cases governments publish data on-line, but under a copyright or "all rights reserved", which by default prohibits any further re-use of these information.[119] Licensing procedures should be adjusted for easy data exchange between stakeholders – business and public bodies (member states in the EU particular case).

- It's still an issue when public bodies publish their data in text or any other non-machine readable format.

In these cases formally data are open, but not prepared for re-use, which makes interoperability an issue. Reasonable question is also: who needs to transform these data into a machine readable format and provide access to it? From which budget should it be paid? Should the requirement of publishing data in machine readable format be implemented only to new data sets or does this also apply for previously published data?

- There is a common idea, that open data is mainly beneficial for big service corporations that know how to

---

[119] Fioretti, M. (2011)" Open Data: Emerging trends, issues and best practices", *Laboratory of Economics and Management of Scuola Superiore Sant'Anna,* Pisa, pp. 13-23

monetize the information rather than for ordinary citizens, who can even be indifferent to these governmental initiatives.[120] [121]

- Linked to the previous issue, this lack of interest from ordinary citizens can make PSI available only to upper classes of society - people, who have better Internet access, modern digital devices and more skills in using online services.

In other words, open data can be one of the reasons of digital exclusion rather than making life of citizens more comfortable. Thus, unequal access and lack of skills and interest to PSI will not bring any effect to this initiative.

- The economic impact of open data strategies implementation still remains vague.[122]

---

[120] Rogers, S. (2011) UK government open data: good bad or dangerous? Tell us what you think, *The Guardian Data Blog*. Available online: http://www.guardian.co.uk/news/datablog/2011/aug/04/uk-government-open-data-maude (Last retrieved 01/11/2012)

[121] Fioretti, M. (2011)" Open Data: Emerging trends, issues and best practices", *Laboratory of Economics and Management of Scuola Superiore Sant'Anna,* Pisa, pp. 3-27

[122] Huijboom, N. & T. Van den Broek (2011) "Open data: an international comparison of strategies", *European Journal of ePractice,* 12 (March/April 2011), pp. 4-15. Available online: http://www.epractice.eu/files/European%20Journal%20epractice%20Volume%2012_4.pdf (Last retrieved 15/08/2012)

As in every innovative situation it's hard to model possible social and economic outcomes, especially if it concerns so many different countries and cities. What works for one place doesn't necessarily fit another place. Also here the question could be raised: should PSI be free of charge for citizens and business or does a government have the right to earn on it or at least cover some marginal costs? According to the Canadian experience, PSI should be free of charge: *"...the total value of public data is maximized when provided for free or where necessary only a minimal cost of distribution ... and when data is shared freely, citizens are enabled to use and re-purpose it to help create a more economically vibrant and environmentally sustainable city"*[123]. The US researchers agree: *"When public sector bodies charge for PSI, those costs can actually inhibit others from adding value. The same is true with licensing restrictions"*[124]. On the other hand, we can look at the issue from a governmental perspective, which should find money to publish, maintain and up-date PSI data on-line preferably in machine readable formats. Again it's the tax

---

[123] City of Hamilton (2011) Notice of Motion, *Open Data Policy*. Available online: http://www.hamilton.ca/NR/rdonlyres/E6C548DD-2FE2-4D21-AF65-B24A2C8BEF2B/0/Aug09EDRMS_n197439_v1_10_1_Notice_of_Motion__Open_Data_Polic.pdf (Last retrieved 01/11/2012)

[124] Uhlir, P.F. (2009) "The Socioeconomic Effects of Public Sector Information on Digital Networks: Toward a Better Understanding of Different Access and Reuse Policies: Workshop Summary", *US National Committee CODATA, in cooperation with OECD,* pp. 10-16.

payer who is covering all these cost to finally enable businesses the chance to make profit out of re-use.

Summary and Conclusions

PSI (public sector information) is data naturally collected and stored by government. Some countries' and cities' authorities make a decision to open it up and let the third parties to use it. Then PSI is becoming an open data. Even though these two concepts (open data and PSI) are not the same things in its cores, in some cases open data and PSI tend to be overlapping notions.

Open Data is a global trend at the moment. More and more governmental bodies and international organizations are interested in opening-up their datasets to get some social and economical benefits out of it. Produced, collected and stored by governmental and public service bodies information are expected to be freely available on-line for other stakeholders as citizens, public organizations and business structures. However, sometimes the matters of interoperability, licensing and structuring datasets becomes difficult. As a result, not all the open data are purely "open".

In spite of some disputable issues around PSI and

controversial moments of its re-use, there are some significant motives for local authorities to open-up their data, mainly in terms of increasing citizen transparency and fostering innovations. Obviously, in every individual city case risks should be measured and balanced with possible benefits. In fact, this "balance point searching" can be the topic of another big research on the concept of "open data".

Chapter 4: Open Data. The legal framework overview

National policy makers are important drivers for open data initiatives development and the process of motivating people to use open data and PSI[125]. Moreover, the lack of political leadership and initiatives to PSI re-use is exactly the reason for the existing blockage of the progress on open data policy. Thus, we find it necessary to make an overview of the current policy framework regarding the PSI domain.

This part of our research is extremely important because it explains indirectly why some cities are "smarter" and more mobile than others. In some territories the implementation of the European legislation on open data goes coherently and with strong support of local authorities. The effect of such a *"willingness to open"* is relatively visible and reflected in launching of new paid and free services in the market (for example: the number of diverse mobile apps for public transport, built on open governmental data). On the contrary, other EU member states are less flexible and even slow in transposing pan-European legislation into their

---

[125] Huijboom, N. & T. Van den Broek (2011) "Open data: an international comparison of strategies", *European Journal of ePractice*, 12 (March/April 2011), pp. 4-15. Available online: http://www.epractice.eu/files/European%20Journal%20epractice%20Volume%2012_4.pdf (Last retrieved 15/08/2012)

national legal frameworks.

Nevertheless, in this Chapter we are not going to speculate and find out the reasons why some European countries are faster and more flexible than others. Our aim is to make an overview of the legitimate open data framework in order to understand the legal basis of this approach.

International framework. OECD - Principles and Guidelines for Access to Research Data from Public Funding (2007)

The first and probably the most general document we want to look at is OECD's (Organization for Economic Co-operation and Development) paper called "Principles and Guidelines for Access to Research Data from Public Funding".

In 2004 in Paris the Organization for Economic Co-operation and Development, consisting of 34 country members (24 out of which are European countries), together with China, Israel, Russia and South Africa adopted a Declaration on Access to Research Data from Public Funding.[126] The paper recognizes the importance of free

---

[126] OECD (2004) "Declaration on Access to Research Data from Public Funding"

public access to all publicly-funded archive data. Later on, in 2006-2007 the OECD also developed and published the Principles and Guidelines for Access to Research Data from Public Funding. [127]

Basically, the paper is recognizing the importance of free public access to all publicly-funded archive data and its main idea can be formulated as: *"The exchange of ideas, knowledge and data emerging is fundamental for human progress and is part of the core of OECD values"*.[128]

The document is based on 13 main principles[129], which are:

- Openness
- Flexibility
- Transparency
- Legal conformity
- Protection of intellectual property

---

[127] OECD (2007) "Principles and Guidelines for Access to Research Data from Public Funding" Available online:
http://www.oecd.org/science/scienceandtechnologypolicy/38500813.pdf (Last retrieved 21/09/2012)

[128] OECD (2007) "Principles and Guidelines for Access to Research Data from Public Funding", p. 3. Available online:
http://www.oecd.org/science/scienceandtechnologypolicy/38500813.pdf (Last retrieved 21/09/2012)

[129] OECD (2007) "Principles and Guidelines for Access to Research Data from Public Funding", pp. 15-22. Available online:
http://www.oecd.org/science/scienceandtechnologypolicy/38500813.pdf (Last retrieved 21/09/2012)

- Formal responsibility
- Professionalism
- Interoperability
- Quality
- Security
- Efficiency
- Accountability
- Sustainability

Moreover, it's emphasized several times in the paper that **data should be digital and interoperable** (*"preferably data should be Internet-based"*, *"ideally through the Internet"*, *"should be easy to find on the Internet"*…etc).

The document is created in a form of recommendations and doesn't have any legal binding status. Anyway, this "soft law" paper actively encourages the OECD member countries take the principles into consideration and implement them in a long standing practice.

The document applies only to publicly-funded archive data and does not damages any privacy low or confidential information: *"Data on human subjects and other personal data are subject to restricted access under national laws and policies to protect confidentiality and privacy"*. [130] However, according to this paper, anonymisation and privacy procedures which guarantee a decent level of confidentiality can be considered to open up for researchers as much valuable data as it possible.

This intergovernmental agreement is more likely the only international document which the EU Member States (at least those who adopted the document) could take into consideration. For the other cases, we clearly can observe strong domination of the European Union legislation. Thus, the biggest part of the Chapter is going to cover this matter.

European Union framework.
Digital Agenda and public data core Directives

Digital Agenda for Europe is a flagship initiative of the EU which was launched in August 2010 and aimed to develop a digital single market in the territory of the European Union. The main standing point of this initiative is the idea that nowadays public, governmental and commercial

---

[130] OECD (2007) "Principles and Guidelines for Access to Research Data from Public Funding", pp. 13-14. Available online: http://www.oecd.org/science/scienceandtechnologypolicy/38500813.pdf (Last retrieved 21/09/2012)

services are moving towards more digitalization and the Union can benefit from this tendency. Therefore, to remain competitive in the world market during a period of economical challenges and at the same time making life of European citizens more comfortable, it is necessary to work on developing new services and particularly on opening up public data.[131]

Among other initiatives declared in this document, the idea of opening up and re-using public sector information (PSI) is clearly noticeable: *"...governments can stimulate content markets by making **public sector information** available on transparent, effective, non-discriminatory terms. This is an important source of potential growth of innovative online services...public bodies must be obliged to open up data resources for cross-border applications and services".*[132]

---

[131] EUROPEAN COMMISSION. COM (2010) 245 final. Communication from the Commission to the European Parliament, the Council, the European Economic and Social Committee and the Committee of the Regions, a Digital Agenda for Europe. 19.5.2010. Available online: http://eur-lex.europa.eu/LexUriServ/LexUriServ.do?uri=COM:2010:0245:FIN:EN:PDF (Last retrieved 15/09/2012)

[132] EUROPEAN COMMISSION. COM (2010) 245 final. Communication from the Commission to the European Parliament, the Council, the European Economic and Social Committee and the Committee of the Regions, a Digital Agenda for Europe. 19.5.2010, p. 7. Available online: http://eur-lex.europa.eu/LexUriServ/LexUriServ.do?uri=COM:2010:0245:FIN:EN:PDF (Last retrieved 15/09/2012)

Later on Neelie Kroes, the Commissioner responsible for the Digital Agenda implementation, more than once has emphasized that opening up governmental data gives a whole new economical, political and social value to the EU society: *"Data is new oil for a digital era"*.[133]

Under the umbrella of the Digital Agenda we can find several Directives, which are the basic tools for the EU authorities to implement the policy around the member states. Referring to public sector information and open data in the context of mobility initiatives we can distinguish two core directives:

1. DIRECTIVE 2003/98/EC OF THE EUROPEAN PARLIAMENT AND OF THE COUNCIL on the re-use of public sector information (of 17 November 2003)

2. DIRECTIVE 2007/2/EC OF THE EUROPEAN PARLIAMENT AND OF THE COUNCIL establishing an Infrastructure for Spatial Information in the European Community (INSPIRE) (of 14 March 2007)

In this Chapter we would like to take a more in depth

---

[133] Kroes, N. (2012) Speech on ePSI conference in Rotterdam March 2012. Available online: http://www.youtube.com/watch?v=9Jq4Qy1UeAE (Last retrieved 03/11/2012)

look into these two directives (shortly – PSI Directive and INSPIRE Directive) as general key drivers of the open data initiative. Its implementation status and specialties of implementation among the Member States will be covered in the next Chapters in the context of cities case studies.

DIRECTIVE 2003/98/EC OF THE EUROPEAN PARLIAMENT AND OF THE COUNCIL on the re-use of public sector information (of 17 November 2003)

Even though the document was launched in 2003, seven years earlier than the Digital Agenda, now it fits the purposes of this initiative and directly refers to the knowledge society and the importance of public sector information as a primary material for digital content products: *"The evolution towards an information and knowledge society influences the life of every citizen in the Community, inter alia, by enabling them to gain new ways of accessing and acquiring knowledge"*. [134]

---

[134] EUROPEAN PARLIAMENT & COUNCIL (2003) DIRECTIVE 2003/98/EC OF THE EUROPEAN PARLIAMENT AND OF THE COUNCIL on the re-use of public sector information (of 17 November 2003), *Official Journal of the European Union* Available online: http://eur-lex.europa.eu/LexUriServ/LexUriServ.do?uri=OJ:L:2003:345:0090:0096:EN:PDF (Last retrieved 12/06/2012)

The Directive (also known as PSI Directive) aims to facilitate the process of re-using public sector information (PSI) in a single digital market by establishing basic re-use conditions, and providing the market with a sufficient legal frame work to do so. [135] The paper is supposed to support the establishment of an internal market, expanding the role of community-wide services in the EU economy. According to the document, data shall be re-usable for commercial or non-commercial purposes, because re-using PSI (as an important primary material for the digital industry) should contribute to the economy and as a result a social growth of the EU. The concept of public sector bodies is based on the idea of public task or *"raison d'être"* for the public sector: *"...established for the specific purpose of meeting needs in the general interest, not having an industrial or commercial character..."*[136] This is why **the idea of**

---

[135] EUROPEAN COMMISSION (2003) Proposal for a DIRECTIVE OF THE EUROPEAN PARLIAMENT AND OF THE COUNCIL, Amending Directive 2003/98/EC on re-use of public sector information Available online:
http://ec.europa.eu/information_society/policy/psi/docs/pdfs/directive_proposal/2012/en.pdf (Last retrieved 08/06/2012)

[136] EUROPEAN PARLIAMENT & COUNCIL (2003) DIRECTIVE 2003/98/EC OF THE EUROPEAN PARLIAMENT AND OF THE COUNCIL on the re-use of public sector information (of 17 November 2003), *Official Journal of the European Union,* Article 2. Available online: http://eur-lex.europa.eu/LexUriServ/LexUriServ.do?uri=OJ:L:2003:345:0090:0096:EN:PDF (Last retrieved 12/06/2012)

wasting some economic potential by not re-using public sector data is the basic idea of the document. In other words, the EU citizens have already paid for collecting and storing all this huge amount of data from their taxes and now these data can and should be re-used for making cities "smarter" and life of its citizens more comfortable.

First of all, the Directive doesn't deal with any data protected by intellectual property rights, copyrights or any kind of national security documents, commercial confidentiality and other private information. It can be applied only to the data (paper documents or sound and audio-visual information), which regional and local governments of the member states are launching on a daily basis.[137]

According to the document, the access to re-use data should be fast (for example for traffic data), because regular up-dates influence the economic value of the usage of this information. According the Directive, as far as the information is already paid off by taxes, whenever possible

---

[137] EUROPEAN PARLIAMENT & COUNCIL (2003) DIRECTIVE 2003/98/EC OF THE EUROPEAN PARLIAMENT AND OF THE COUNCIL on the re-use of public sector information (of 17 November 2003), *Official Journal of the European Union,* Article 2. Available online: http://eur-lex.europa.eu/LexUriServ/LexUriServ.do?uri=OJ:L:2003:345:0090:0096:EN:PDF (Last retrieved 12/06/2012)

PSI should be re-used by third parties free of charge or at least not more than marginal costs: *"Where charges are made, the total income from supplying and allowing re-use of documents shall not exceed the cost of collection, production, reproduction and dissemination, together with a reasonable return on investment."*[138]

In addition to this statement, the conditions of "non-discrimination" policy should be observed: *"The re-use of documents shall be open to all potential actors in the market, even if one or more market players already exploit added-value products based on these documents. Contracts or other arrangements between the public sector bodies holding the documents and third parties shall not grant exclusive rights."*[139] In other words, every public body, private company or citizen should have equal rights to get the data.

Public sector bodies should also make data available in formats, applicable for electronic needs or machine-

---

[138] EUROPEAN PARLIAMENT & COUNCIL (2003) DIRECTIVE 2003/98/EC OF THE EUROPEAN PARLIAMENT AND OF THE COUNCIL on the re-use of public sector information (of 17 November 2003), *Official Journal of the European Union,* Article 6. Available online: http://eur-lex.europa.eu/LexUriServ/LexUriServ.do?uri=OJ:L:2003:345:0090:0096:EN:PDF (Last retrieved 12/06/2012)

[139] EUROPEAN PARLIAMENT & COUNCIL (2003) DIRECTIVE 2003/98/EC OF THE EUROPEAN PARLIAMENT AND OF THE COUNCIL on the re-use of public sector information (of 17 November 2003), *Official Journal of the European Union,* Article 11. Available online: http://eur-lex.europa.eu/LexUriServ/LexUriServ.do?uri=OJ:L:2003:345:0090:0096:EN:PDF (Last retrieved 12/06/2012)

readable: *"Where possible, documents shall be made available through electronic means."*[140]

As the main basics of the PSI Directive are "transparency and a fair competition"[141], the legal process of re-using PSI in the territory of the EU is the following: national public sector authorities process requests of stakeholders (citizens, commercial and non-commercial organizations) and make PSI available on-line preferably in machine-readable formats. In case of licensing, it should take not more than 20 days for a public body to explain to an applicant the requirements. In case it's impossible to open-up public sector body's data, this organization should give reasons why information is closed. When any payments or charges are needed to share the data, the public sector body, , shouldn't exceed marginal costs (costs of production, collection and distribution). Moreover, these charging

---

[140] EUROPEAN PARLIAMENT & COUNCIL (2003) DIRECTIVE 2003/98/EC OF THE EUROPEAN PARLIAMENT AND OF THE COUNCIL on the re-use of public sector information (of 17 November 2003), *Official Journal of the European Union,* Article 3. Available online: http://eur-lex.europa.eu/LexUriServ/LexUriServ.do?uri=OJ:L:2003:345:0090:0096:EN:PDF (Last retrieved 12/06/2012)

[141] Fornefeld, M. & G. Boele-Keimer, S. Recher, M. Fanning (2008) "Assessment of the Re-use of Public Sector Information (PSI) in the Geographical information, Meteorological Information and Legal Information Sectors", Final report, *MICUS Management Consulting GmbH,* Düsseldorf. Available online: http://ec.europa.eu/information_society/policy/psi/docs/pdfs/micus_report_december2008.pdf (Last retrieved 01/11/2012)

conditions should be pre-presented and published. Thus, the competition should be non-discriminatory and the information has to be available for all the interested stakeholders under the equal rules and conditions. Exclusive arrangements are prohibited. In fact, all this primary minimum of rules can, and preferably should be expended and improved by member states, as long as the Directive sets only the minimum recommendations.

It's important to note that previously the questions of open data regulations were ruled specifically according to the member states regulation. After the entering into the force the PSI Directive on 31 December 2003, open data regulation officially became a legislative act of the European Union.

The Directive is built above the Member States rules concerning the access to information and doesn't have the purpose to damage it. In fact, it can only encourage, by a minimum set of rules, the EU member states to make public sector information available for private and public organizations as well as for citizens.

Although the PSI Directive was not fully transposed into the all Member States national legislations until 2008, it has some optimistic moves within the EU. According to some resent researches, re-use of PSI is increasing, especially in the sector of geographical information.[142]

The Directive was not fully transposed by all member states until the official deadline – 2008, but by July 2010, all 27 EU members notified the Commission about factual implementation of the PSI Directive rules into their national legislation. The next review of the PSI Directive was planned by 2012, thus in December 2011 the Commission launched a co-called "Open Data Package" which includes:

- a Communication on open data:
- a Proposal for a revision of the Directive
- new Commission rules on re-use of the documents

In June 2009 the PSI Directive was reviewed. The Commission examined the way in which the EU PSI rules had been applied. As a result, the Commission confirmed that PSI re-usage had been growing, but to use the full potential of PSI for the EU economy, EU Member States had to remove some still remaining barriers and also emphasize that the situation in the European Union is in clear contrast with

---

[142] Fornefeld, M. & G. Boele-Keimer, S. Recher, M. Fanning (2008) "Assessment of the Re-use of Public Sector Information (PSI) in the Geographical information, Meteorological Information and Legal Information Sectors", Final report, *MICUS Management Consulting GmbH*, Düsseldorf. Available online:
http://ec.europa.eu/information_society/policy/psi/docs/pdfs/micus_report_december2008.pdf (Last retrieved 01/11/2012)

the US, where re-use is strongly encouraged.[143] Hence, according to this review document, Member States should take further steps to use the whole potential of PSI for the EU economy. According to the Commission clarification, the situation in the EU is in clear contrast with the US, where re-use is strongly encouraged. [144]

In 2010 the Commission arranged some consultations with interested parties (citizens, academics, public authorities, etc.)[145] According to these consultations, the Commission concluded that people are not really supporting charging for PSI and think it should be free for non-commercial re-use. they complained that public sector information should also be accessable across the Union borders, which is fully

---

[143] EUROPEAN COMMISSION (2009) COMMUNICATION FROM THE COMMISSION TO THE EUROPEAN PARLIAMENT, THE COUNCIL, THE EUROPEAN ECONOMIC AND SOCIAL COMMITTEE AND THE COMMITTEE OF THE REGIONS Re-use of Public Sector Information – Review of Directive 2003/98/EC – 2009/2011)

[144] Fornefeld, M. & G. Boele-Keimer, S. Recher, M. Fanning (2008) "Assessment of the Re-use of Public Sector Information (PSI) in the Geographical information, Meteorological Information and Legal Information Sectors", Final report, *MICUS Management Consulting GmbH*, Düsseldorf. Available online: http://ec.europa.eu/information_society/policy/psi/docs/pdfs/micus_report_december2008.pdf (Last retrieved 01/11/2012)

[145] Kronenburg, T. (2011) "Differences in the 2008 and 2010 public online consultations regarding the PSI Directive", Topic Report No. 2011/8, *European Public Sector Information Platform.* Available online: http://ru.scribd.com/doc/106896070/Topic-Report-Differences-Public-Consultations (Last retrieved 06/11/2012)

supporting the idea of a digital single market, emphasized in the Digital Agenda. The principle when the public bodies should not be allowed to charge more than marginal costs was established and highly encouraged.

In the Legislative proposal of the document (2011), the Commission proposes co-called *"Impact assessment"*, which suggests five possible options on the PSI legislation development. [146] **The first option** assumes no policy changes, remaining the Directive the way it is. **The second option** is rather radical. It suggests discontinuing of the PSI Directive. This basically means that without this document Member States can still be free to revise their own national implementing legislation for public sector information re-use., this option could mean that it will be only the Member States themselves who are responsible for opening up and processing all the PSI on their jurisdiction without reporting to the Commission. **The third option**, which the Commission has proposed in the revision of the Directive is kind of a "soft law" measure where the EU official body can only guide and give recommendations to the Member States.

---

[146] EUROPEAN COMMISSION (2011) Legislative proposal 2011/0430(COD) - 12/12/2011. Available online: http://www.europarl.europa.eu/oeil/popups/summary.do?id=1181131&t=d&l=en (Last retrieved 06/11/2012)

This consultancy, according to the option, can concern supervision on some technical issues (for example: formats and interoperability matters) and financial issues (for example: price calculations or marginal costs estimations). **Option number four** implies lawmaking amendments which basically could turn the legislation to some new areas. As to these amendments we can refer for example an *"extension of the scope of the Directive to currently excluded sectors (cultural, educational and research establishments as well as public"*. Another quite visible action could be *"imposing a requirement to publish data in machine-readable formats"*[147]

The last proposed option, **option number five** is called "Packaged solution" which basically combines options #3 and #4 - guidelines and recommendations from the Commission to the Members States on technical and financial issues with some legislative amendments in terms of the current Directive extension.

According to the Legislative proposal paper, exactly option #4 offers the best balance between developing the idea of the re-using of PSI and its legal harmonization with national law specificities.

---

[147] EUROPEAN COMMISSION (2011) Legislative proposal 2011/0430(COD) - 12/12/2011. Available online: http://www.europarl.europa.eu/oeil/popups/summary.do?id=1181131&t=d&l=en (Last retrieved 06/11/2012)

According to the Commission Communication on open data, minimum harmonization in PSI didn't resolve the problem of differences in the member states law and, as a result, development of cross-border information services. One of the biggest issues is monopolistic tendencies on open data keeping. Thus, the main conclusion is: "At the moment, its full potential is far from being realized" and more steps to opening-up public sector information should be done by both sides: the Commission and the member states.

The proposals for a revision of the Directive[148]:

• to include new PSI bodies (public and university libraries, museums and archives)
• to limit the fees for PSI re-use by the marginal costs
• to make data interoperable and machine-readable

Now the "Open Data Package" documents and the text of the Directive itself are the official papers for the

---

[148] EUROPEAN COMMISSION (2003) Proposal for a DIRECTIVE OF THE EUROPEAN PARLIAMENT AND OF THE COUNCIL, Amending Directive 2003/98/EC on re-use of public sector information Available online: http://ec.europa.eu/information_society/policy/psi/docs/pdfs/directive_proposal/2012/en.pdf (Last retrieved 08/06/2012)

Member States to operate in the legislative framework. Basically, the Commission has now made its proposals and it will take up to 2 years for the Member States to finally agree and implement the text.

DIRECTIVE 2007/2/EC OF THE EUROPEAN PARLIAMENT AND OF THE COUNCIL establishing an Infrastructure for Spatial Information in the European Community (INSPIRE) (of 14 March 2007)

The INSPIRE Directive[149] was adopted by the EU on the 14th of March 2007 and entered into force on the 15th of May 2007. Full implementation of the document is required by all the Member States by 2019. The document was launched to create a pan-European spatial data infrastructure to facilitate the sharing of environmental spatial information among public sector bodies across the EU and make public access to spatial information across Europe easier.

---

[149] EUROPEAN PARLIAMENT & COUNCIL (2007) DIRECTIVE 2007/2/EC OF THE EUROPEAN PARLIAMENT AND OF THE COUNCIL establishing an Infrastructure for Spatial Information in the European Community (INSPIRE) (of 14 March 2007), *Official Journal of the European Union*. Available online: http://eur-lex.europa.eu/LexUriServ/LexUriServ.do?uri=OJ:L:2007:108:0001:0014:EN:PDF (Last retrieved 08/06/2012)

The INSPIRE Directive doesn't deal with any data protected by intellectual property rights, copyrights or any kind of national security documents, commercial confidentiality and other private information. *"This Directive does not affect the existence or ownership of public authorities' intellectual property rights".* [150] The document can be applied only to the geo-special data, which regional and local governments of the Member States launches.

The Directive addresses 34 spatial data themes[151] needed for environmental applications (geology, transport networks, area management, utility governmental services etc.) and in a particular refers to air, water, soil and natural landscape data.

The main idea of the paper is that the infrastructure for spatial data should be established on

---

[150] EUROPEAN PARLIAMENT & COUNCIL (2007) DIRECTIVE 2007/2/EC OF THE EUROPEAN PARLIAMENT AND OF THE COUNCIL establishing an Infrastructure for Spatial Information in the European Community (INSPIRE) (of 14 March 2007), *Official Journal of the European Union*, Article 2. Available online: http://eur-lex.europa.eu/LexUriServ/LexUriServ.do?uri=OJ:L:2007:108:0001:0014:EN:PDF (Last retrieved 08/06/2012)

[151] EUROPEAN PARLIAMENT & COUNCIL (2007) DIRECTIVE 2007/2/EC OF THE EUROPEAN PARLIAMENT AND OF THE COUNCIL establishing an Infrastructure for Spatial Information in the European Community (INSPIRE) (of 14 March 2007), *Official Journal of the European Union*, Annex I,II,III. Available online: http://eur-lex.europa.eu/LexUriServ/LexUriServ.do?uri=OJ:L:2007:108:0001:0014:EN:PDF (Last retrieved 08/06/2012)

pan-European level. Thus, in all the member states spatial data should be collected, stored, maintained and made available in the most appropriate way to use it across the EU. In addition, member states should provide data through the EU with the help of a special INSPIRE geo-portal operated by the Commission.

Taking into account regional and local differences and situations in different Member States of the EU, the coordination between them is needed. Thus, formats and the structure of the data should be interoperable and based on the international standards. To provide Member States with tools for interoperability, the document proposes to establish a special web-site, geoportal: *"The Commission shall establish and operate an Inspire geoportal at Community level"* [152]

A lot of attention is paid to the importance of making the data interoperable, because the main purpose of the initiative is smooth using all this data across the EU: " …*'interoperability' means the possibility for spatial data sets to be combined, and for services to interact, without repetitive manual*

---

[152] EUROPEAN PARLIAMENT & COUNCIL (2007) DIRECTIVE 2007/2/EC OF THE EUROPEAN PARLIAMENT AND OF THE COUNCIL establishing an Infrastructure for Spatial Information in the European Community (INSPIRE) (of 14 March 2007), *Official Journal of the European Union*, Article 15. Available online: http://eur-lex.europa.eu/LexUriServ/LexUriServ.do?uri=OJ:L:2007:108:0001:0014:EN:PDF (Last retrieved 08/06/2012)

intervention, in such a way that the result is coherent and the added value of the data sets and services is enhanced..."[153] or *"...organisations established under international law have adopted relevant standards to ensure interoperability or harmonisation of spatial data sets and services, these standards shall be integrated..."*[154]

according to the document, the minimum number of services should be available free of charge: *"Member States shall ensure that the services referred to in points (a) and (b) of Article 11(1) are available to the public free of charge"*[155] in spite of it *"This*

---

[153] EUROPEAN PARLIAMENT & COUNCIL (2007) DIRECTIVE 2007/2/EC OF THE EUROPEAN PARLIAMENT AND OF THE COUNCIL establishing an Infrastructure for Spatial Information in the European Community (INSPIRE) (of 14 March 2007), *Official Journal of the European Union*, Article 3. Available online: http://eur-lex.europa.eu/LexUriServ/LexUriServ.do?uri=OJ:L:2007:108:0001:0014:EN:PDF (Last retrieved 08/06/2012)

[154] EUROPEAN PARLIAMENT & COUNCIL (2007) DIRECTIVE 2007/2/EC OF THE EUROPEAN PARLIAMENT AND OF THE COUNCIL establishing an Infrastructure for Spatial Information in the European Community (INSPIRE) (of 14 March 2007), *Official Journal of the European Union*, Article 7. Available online: http://eur-lex.europa.eu/LexUriServ/LexUriServ.do?uri=OJ:L:2007:108:0001:0014:EN:PDF (Last retrieved 08/06/2012)

[155] EUROPEAN PARLIAMENT & COUNCIL (2007) DIRECTIVE 2007/2/EC OF THE EUROPEAN PARLIAMENT AND OF THE COUNCIL establishing an Infrastructure for Spatial Information in the European Community (INSPIRE) (of 14 March 2007), *Official Journal of the European Union*, Article 14. Available online: http://eur-lex.europa.eu/LexUriServ/LexUriServ.do?uri=OJ:L:2007:108:0001:0014:EN:PDF (Last retrieved 08/06/2012)

Directive does not require collection of new spatial data".[156]

In fact, the INSPIRE Directive is aimed to assist some policy-making process in issues of spatial information services across Europe, but also this document has a clear potential for smart cities development. Based on open air, water, soil and natural landscape data the Member States governments and pan-European organizations have the ability to create new diverse environmental applications concerning transport networks, area management, geology issues, utility governmental services etc.

Correspondence of two Directives

The Commission invites the EU Member States to adopt "re-use" and "geo-spatial data" sharing policies as early as possible. Hence, some countries are not in a hurry while others have launched their own programs under these two Directives to implement the documents smoothly. A more in

---

[156] EUROPEAN PARLIAMENT & COUNCIL (2007) DIRECTIVE 2007/2/EC OF THE EUROPEAN PARLIAMENT AND OF THE COUNCIL establishing an Infrastructure for Spatial Information in the European Community (INSPIRE) (of 14 March 2007), *Official Journal of the European Union*, Article 4. Available online: http://eur-lex.europa.eu/LexUriServ/LexUriServ.do?uri=OJ:L:2007:108:0001:0014:EN:PDF (Last retrieved 08/06/2012)

depth view on these specific governmental initiatives is provided in the case studies Chapter of this paper.

Going back to two basic public data Directives (PSI Directive and INSPIRE Directive) it seems essential to say some words about the way these documents correspond to each other. First of all, **both papers argue that the right to knowledge is a basic principle of democracy, so public data should be open for easy access to citizens**. Secondly, the importance of opening up data for economical reasons is highly emphasized in the PSI Directive while the importance of interoperability of data is more covered in the INSPIRE Directive text. At the same time, both directives actively promote the idea of re-using and sharing data free of charge or at least not exceeding the marginal costs.

Summary and Conclusions

To understand the process of open data initiative implementation and evaluate the results of this approach in different EU Member States, we first should look at the legal framework of the issue in all the possible levels: from global, through the EU down to the national Member States.

The PSI Directive and INSPIRE Directive are general

key drivers of open data initiatives in the European Union. Even though these two documents have different primary motivations, both papers support the idea of re-using and sharing data free of charge or at least not exceeding the marginal costs. The PSI Directive is mainly based on economic reasons and the potential values of re-using public sector information for the Member States economy, while the INSPIRE Directive promotes the significance of interoperability of data within the EU. According to both documents, re-using of public data is a basis for a digital age, thus data shall be re-usable and interoperable across the EU borders.

Part 2: Empirical research
Chapter 5: Case studies London, Berlin, Brussels

Motivation of choice and research methodology

The principles of selection were based first of all on the "capital" status of the cities and, second of all on the relevantly large size of the megapolices. All three cities are big financial, political and social centers of the European Union. Moreover, these three cases are spread around the EU area, which made us suggest that the approaches of the cities to the ICT practices implementation into the urban environment could be different. In addition, the availability of the information about the cases in English was an important factor, even though some of the original documents we also processed in French and German.

Every case is analyzed by the same set of parameters. First of all, a local transport system overview is made to understand who (which organization) is the "data owner" and decision-maker of the urban mobility in the chosen area is. This overview also helps to understand the scale and the structure of the existing mobility case. The next parameter we looked at is the EU open data regulation implementation. In the previous Chapters of the thesis we discussed some legal data issues in the EU area, so we found it important to analyze the real implementation of the policy. The last but not the least parameter we looked at is the overview of apps for urban mobility in every particular case. In one case all the ICT solutions can be purely based on open data, in the other cases we see that apps are developed with other alternative sources of mobility (crowd-sourcing, Twitter etc.). The analysis was based on the official documents and researches available online as well as on a number of other open and reliable web recourses as national and regional data stores and databases.

In the end of the case studies research we compared all three cases on the agreed set of parameters and made the conclusions of what the urban mobility in the EU looks like and what still can be improved.

Except of the policy analyses, we created a data base of the mobile applications available in the three cities of the case studies. Furthermore, the expert interview method helped us to fill some gaps in the understanding of every particular case. Even though the experts' interview is classified as a separate Chapter, we find its results obviously relevant to use in the case studies part of the research.

The full mobile apps database and the interviews transcripts can be found in the Appendix.

CASE STUDY №1. City of London

The public transport system

The City of London public transport network is one of the most widespread and busy megapolis systems in the world. It's regulated by a statutory corporation - Transport for London (TfL), which members are appointed directly by the mayor of the city. The TfL is divided in three main directorates:

1) London Underground (city metro or "tube")

2) London Rail (suburban rails, light railways and trams)

3) Surface transport (buses, black cabs, public bicycle service etc.)

As an alternative way of urban mobility, in the summer of 2010 the city authorities also have begun to develop the municipal system of cycling. Approximately 6,000 bicycles at 400 stations in nine central London districts are available for short-term rental.[157]

As an international business, financial and cultural centre, the City of London is forced to optimize the public transport system. The nearest traffic challenge for the local administration is related with the preparation for the summer Olympic Games 2012 (27/07/12 – 12/08/2012). [158] [159]

Most of the decisions concerning public transport system development are technical or classically urban by its nature, but recent ICT technologies are also designed to help the modern megapolis to become more mobile and comfortable for citizens and visitors.

---

[157] The official website of the City of London, City transport policies. Available online: http://www.cityoflondon.gov.uk/Corporation/LGNL_Services/Transport_and_streets/Transport_policy/strategic_transport.htm (Last retrieved 17/11/2012)

[158] The official website of the London Olympic Games 2012. Available online: http://www.london2012.com/making-it-happen/transport/index.php (Last retrieved 17/11/2012)

[159] Rogers, S. (2012) London 2012: is this the first open data Olympics? The Guardian Data blog, 03/08/2012. Available online: http://www.guardian.co.uk/commentisfree/2012/aug/03/london-2012-olympics-open-data (Last retrieved 04/11/2012)

Legislative framework
PSI Directive implementation

By 8 May 2008 the PSI Directive (DIRECTIVE 2003/98/EC OF THE EUROPEAN PARLIAMENT AND OF THE COUNCIL on the re-use of public sector information (of 17 November 2003))[160] was transposed to the UK national law by adopting explicit PSI re-use measures and launching a new legislative instrument - "The Re-use of public sector information regulations of 10/06/2005, Her Majesty's Stationery Office (HMSO) n° 1515 of 01/07/2005"[161]

Specifically, a "Public Sector Body" term was defined and the list of the exact PSB existing in the territory of the UK was presented in Article 3. Apparently, the public transport organizations can be a part of this classification:

---

[160] EUROPEAN PARLIAMENT & COUNCIL (2003) DIRECTIVE 2003/98/EC OF THE EUROPEAN PARLIAMENT AND OF THE COUNCIL on the re-use of public sector information (of 17 November 2003), *Official Journal of the European Union* Available online: http://eur-lex.europa.eu/LexUriServ/LexUriServ.do?uri=OJ:L:2003:345:0090:0096:EN:PDF (Last retrieved 12/06/2012)

[161] The Minister for the Cabinet Office (2005) No. 1515, PUBLIC SECTOR INFORMATION
The Re-use of Public Sector Information Regulations, Available online: http://www.legislation.gov.uk/uksi/2005/1515/pdfs/uksi_20051515_en.pdf (Last retrieved 10/06/2012)

"(w) a corporation established or a group of individuals appointed to act together for the specific purposes of meeting needs in the general interest, not having an industrial or commercial character, and— (i) financed wholly or mainly by another public sector body, or (ii) subject to management supervision by another public sector body, or (iii) more than half of the board of directors or members of which, or, in the case of a group of individuals, more than half of those individuals, are appointed by another public sector body"[162]

Furthermore, a definition to "re-use" was given in the Article 4: *"...the use by a person of a document held by a public sector body for a purpose other than the initial purpose within that public sector body's public task for which the document was produced".* [163] In the Article 15 it's said that *"A public sector body may charge for allowing re-use",* but not exceeding marginal costs (costs of collection, production, reproduction and dissemination of data). Looking ahead a bit, we would say that nowadays most of the public sector information datasets in the UK are free for non-commercial as well as for commercial use under the "Open

Government License for PSI" regulation.[164]

Non-discrimination policy and prohibition of exclusive arrangements stated in the PSI Directive are respected in the UK legislative act as well.

INSPIRE Directive implementation

In this period, the United Kingdom is probably the European country where open data are getting the most attention from central government and major national parties.

The INSPIRE Directive[165] was transposed into UK legislation on 31 December 2009. Moreover, *"... in December 2009 the government outlined plans in a paper titled "Smarter Government" for England to improve its services, increase efficiency, and*

---

[164] The official website of the UK Government, Open public license for PSI. Available online: http://www.nationalarchives.gov.uk/doc/open-government-licence/ (Last retrieved 10/06/2012)
[165] EUROPEAN PARLIAMENT & COUNCIL (2007) DIRECTIVE 2007/2/EC OF THE EUROPEAN PARLIAMENT AND OF THE COUNCIL establishing an Infrastructure for Spatial Information in the European Community (INSPIRE) (of 14 March 2007), *Official Journal of the European Union*. Available online: http://eur-lex.europa.eu/LexUriServ/LexUriServ.do?uri=OJ:L:2007:108:0001:0014:EN:PDF (Last retrieved 08/06/2012)

use technology to help get better value for money from its assets".[166]

In 2008 the Government of the United Kingdom has launched a special plan, a pan-government initiative called **"The UK Location Programme"** which main aim is to implement the EU INSPIRE Directive in a proper way by improving the sharing and re-using of public sector location information. Thus, we could say that "The UK Location Programme" was tailored to create a kind of synergy with INSPIRE and manage the process of opening PSI smoothly. This is why we should look at these two documents, the INSPIRE Directive and "The UK Location Programme" as well as to the PSI Directive of the European Commission, as a whole system of the UK governmental support for open data innovations: *"Implementation of the Location Strategy will maximize the value to the public, government and UK industry of the use of geographical information. It will provide a consistent framework to assist national, regional and local initiatives, and service delivery for the benefit of all our people"*.[167]

---

[166] UK Location Programme Team (2010) "UNITED KINGDOM 2010, INSPIRE Monitoring and Reporting". Available online: http://location.defra.gov.uk/wp-content/uploads/2009/11/UK-INSPIRE-REPORT-2010-v1-3.pdf (Last retrieved 17/11/2012)

[167] Geographic Information Panel (2008) *Report to Baroness Andrews, Minister for Geographic Information Panel*, Communities and Local Government. Available online: http://location.defra.gov.uk/wp-content/uploads/2009/12/uk-location-strategy.pdf (Last retrieved 17/11/2012)

The main idea was to open PSI datasets as much as possible and to encourage entrepreneurs to re-use this open data information. The government has decided that the process of sharing PSI data across the country was so ineffective, that people and the official bodies were simply wasting time and money trying to find all this information. The proposal was to improve the sharing opportunities through common interoperability standards and common web-infrastructure (web-site in these terms). According to this initiative all the data should be up-dated regularly.

Citizens and community are encouraged to create and develop new PC and mobile applications or to improve already existing government services. [168] At the same moment, governmental departments are encouraged to open their PSI. There is a guide which demonstrates how to publish data easily. Assistance in the web-site forum is also provided.[169] The authorities also give some suggestions for potential apps based on all these PSI. Traffic management, location based services, social-economic services are mentioned as possible apps solutions. Even though the

---

[168] The official website of the UK Government. Available online: http://data.gov.uk/ (Last retrieved 12/11/2012)

[169] The official website of the UK Government. Local Spending Data Guidance. Available online: http://data.gov.uk/blog/local-spending-data-guidance (Last retrieved 17/11/2012)

INSPIRE Directive does not force members states to create some extra datasets or launch any national geo-portal, the UK came up with an initiative to do so.

According to the Commission rules on the INSPIRE Directive implementation, the EU Member States have to report yearly concerning the achievements on the paper. The last reports on every member states were done in 2011 and refer to 2010. [170] According to this paper, the UK Location Programme is positively going towards full implementation of the INSPIRE Directive during the next 10 years in line with the official timescales implementation of the Directive. The next important stage the UK government sees, is to work on better data standardization. Obviously, "The UK Location Programme" is at an early stage, but according to the official UK report, this EU member state is planning to implement the INSPIRE Directive in line with "The UK Location Programme" initiatives during the next 10 years by *"coordination and governance mechanisms and building the central*

---

[170] The European Commission official website, INSPIRE Monitoring & Reporting. Available online:
http://inspire.jrc.ec.europa.eu/index.cfm/pageid/182/list/indicators/y/2011/sel/2 (Last retrieved 17/11/2012)

infrastructure for data standardization. [171]

In June 2010 the data.gov.uk team announced the first meeting of a new "Public Sector Transparency Board" to:

- make "transparency" as a primary principle of the government functioning
- be sure that the deadlines for opening-up the most important public datasets are respected
- set common open data standards, according to the principle that: *"Public data policy and practice will be clearly driven by the public and businesses who want and use the data, including what data is released when and in what form."* [172]

"Open Data White Paper"

In the end of June 2012, the UK government has published a new document "Open Data White Paper", emphasizing the idea that "Transparency is at the heart of the

---

[171] UK Location Programme Team (2010) "UNITED KINGDOM 2010, INSPIRE Monitoring and Reporting". Available online: http://location.defra.gov.uk/wp-content/uploads/2009/11/UK-INSPIRE-REPORT-2010-v1-3.pdf (Last retrieved 17/11/2012)

[172] The official website of the UK Government. Available online: http://data.gov.uk/ (Last retrieved 12/11/2012)

agenda for the government."[173] http://www.cabinetoffice.gov.uk/resource-library/open-data-white-paper-unleashing-potential The principle of the UK government is formulated as "data that can be published should be published" and it distinguishes the UK and the "London case" in particular.

This is why each governmental department of the UK (from the Department for Environment, Food and Rural Affairs to the Department for Culture Media and Sport, a total of 14) took this principle as a primary rule and published its first ever Open Data Strategies plans to open up and publish new datasets in the next two years. Departments also stated how they are going to motivate the market for open data use.

The UK Departments which launched their own open data strategies: [174]

---

[173] Cabinet Office of the UK (2012) Open Data White Paper: Unleashing the Potential. Available online: http://www.cabinetoffice.gov.uk/sites/default/files/resources/CM8353_acc.pdf (Last retrieved 17/11/2012)

[174] The official website of the Cabinet Office, Open Data White Paper and Departmental Open Data Strategies. Available online: http://www.cabinetoffice.gov.uk/content/open-data-white-paper-and-

- Home Office (HO)
- Cabinet Office (CO)
- Department for Environment, Food and Rural Affairs (DEFRA)
- Department of Energy & Climate Change (DECC)
- Department for Education (DfE)
- Foreign & Commonwealth Office (FCO)
- Her Majesty's Treasury (HMT)
- Ministry of Defence (MoD)
- Business, Innovation & Skills (BIS)
- Department for International Development (DfID)
- Department for Culture Media and Sport (DCMS)
- Department for Health (DOH)
- HM Revenue & Customs (HMRC)
- Department for Transport

According to the paper and an additional plan - the "Open Data Strategy Annex Summary"[175] some of the departments by opening-up their datasets allow public and business bodies to: *"...copy, publish, distribute and transmit the*

---

departmental-open-data-strategies (Last retrieved 17/11/2012)

[175] Cabinet Office of the UK (2012) Open Data White Paper: Unleashing the Potential, pp. 47-51. Available online: http://www.cabinetoffice.gov.uk/sites/default/files/resources/CM8353_acc.pdf (Last retrieved 17/11/2012)

Information; adapt the Information; exploit the Information commercially for example, by combining it with other Information, or by including it in their own product or application". The general public and businesses can do it for free, simply by using special licenses. [176]

Basically, giving the "Open Government License for PSI" means that citizens, non-commercial and even commercial organizations can copy, publish, distribute, transmit and adapt presented datasets, as well as utilize it commercially, including the possibility to combine it with other datasets and put it in their own products and services. The main condition is to attribute the source of information and give a link to "Open Government License for PSI" itself. Anyhow, the License doesn't cover any personal data or any information under the intellectual property rights law. Furthermore, no organization providing the data (The Information Provider) can give a guarantee of the continued supply of the data.

The authors of the "Open Data White Paper" also believe that proper and supportive legislation and standardization of data are the key factors for supporting an

---

[176] The official website of the UK Government, Open public license for PSI. Available online: http://www.nationalarchives.gov.uk/doc/open-government-licence/ (Last retrieved 10/06/2012)

effective ecosystem. It is stated that opening-up datasets is not enough effort to make the system work. One more important condition to a successful open data strategy implementation is the encouragement and motivation of citizens to use the information in their everyday life and for developers to exploit full business potential and generate added value out of open data.

The paper highly supports privacy and data security policies, stressing that anonymous datasets will remain this way and personal sensitive data will stay personal in any case. Finally, the authors of the "Open Data White Paper" proclaim that a shift to more personalization on data sharing issues in public services domains is needed.

Overview of applications for urban mobility in the City of London

Open data initiatives are performed in the UK on both levels - national[177] and city level[178]. Public data is available and it is quite easy to find all the datasets through a

---

[177] The official website of the UK Government. Available online: http://data.gov.uk/ (Last retrieved 12/11/2012)
[178] The official website of City of London. Available online: http://data.london.gov.uk/ (Last retrieved 12/11/2012)

single online portal: *"www.data.gov.uk"*. At the moment there are about 9,000 datasets available, from all central government departments and some public sector bodies and local authorities[179]. All these data are available on the official web-sites and free to use. Navigation in the national open data web-site is quite easy. Except published data sets, potential users can find all the applications (based on these data) by key words, topics or tags.[180]

On the city web-site mobile applications are not shown in a separate group, but on this on-line recourse we can easily find all datasets opened by local administration. The categories are:

- Art and Culture

- Business and Economy

- Championing London

- Crime and Community Safety

- Demographics

---

[179] Cabinet Office of the UK (2012) Open Data White Paper: Unleashing the Potential. Available online: http://www.cabinetoffice.gov.uk/sites/default/files/resources/CM8353_acc.pdf (Last retrieved 17/11/2012)

[180] The official website of the UK Government, Open Data Applications. Available online: http://data.gov.uk/apps (Last retrieved 12/11/2012)

- Education

- Employment and Skills

- Environment

- Health

- Housing

- London 2012

- Planning

- Sport

- Transparency

- Transport

- Young People

The transport category is one of the biggest in this list and consists of 43 different datasets. Some of them are more popular, some of them – less. It can be evaluated by the number of comments and feedbacks on every dataset. All these data are open under special terms and conditions and free to use.[181]

---

[181] The official website of the Transport for London, Transport data service. Available online:

To our research we have filtered only those applications, which reference to urban mobility issues and created specifically to mobile phones (see Appendix). Using these official sources of information (both: national and city levels) as well as using the most popular digital application platforms for iOS (AppStore), Android (Android Market), Windows (Windows Marketplace)and Blackberry (Blackberry App World), we have created the list of mobile applications which are supposed to help ordinary citizens with their mobility matters. The list is not intended to be complete. We even believe that it is extending constantly and by the end of working on this paper the number of available mobile applications for the City of London will grow.

When observing existing mobile applications we can clearly indicate tendencies distinguishing this city case from the others cases. First of all in the "London case" all 19 applications we have found are purely based on open data information. If we compare this with the other EU member states capitals, we will see that the city has made a great progress in re-using PSI. Our quick-scan allows for the idea that the UK government is probably one of the most enthused European official bodies in terms of opening its

---

http://www.tfl.gov.uk/termsandconditions/11402.aspx (Last retrieved 17/11/2012)

datasets.

The first type of mobile apps we would like to observe are **public transport applications**. London datasets on public transport allow third parties developers to create mobile apps that are able to show the locations of underground and over ground routes and services. Data is officially provided by the TfL organization and can also be available for any user in a desktop regime.[182]

---

[182] The official website of the Transport for London, Live bus departures. Available online: http://countdown.tfl.gov.uk/#/ (Last retrieved 17/11/2012)

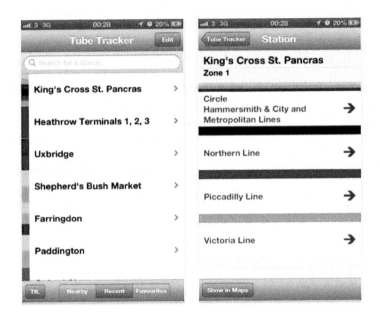

Tube Tracker iOS application, Jetpack Studios LLP

Mobile applications, based on live departure boards and updated bus and tram timetables allow to track bus, tram and tube journeys and observe how many minutes are left until a transport arrives. A time of first and last buses is also available. Through GPS navigators, integrated into smart phones, it's also possible to indicate the nearest bus stops where a person using the app is standing. Some of these mobile apps are also equipped with the function of "notification". It means that the app can inform a user when he or she need to came out of the house (or any other location) to be in a public transport stop in time. The only thing that is needed, is to save the information about a "favorite" route in the app.

Except the city navigation information and the public transport locations, we would also identify a popularity of **"bicycles location" apps** and **"traffic control by street cameras" apps**.

There are around 170 live traffic cameras across the City of London, which are showing what's happening in the capital's streets and if any traffic congestions or accidents occur.[183] This dataset was released by the British government in January of 2010 and some of the developers have used it to create free and paid apps for the city mobility. In our research tables we identified these apps as "Traffic control through using cameras on the streets" (see Appendix). A user can find the needed camera location on the integrated app map. Images are refreshing every three minutes and have special date and time-stamps. Sustainable internet connection is required.

---

[183] The official website of the London Datastore, TfL Live Traffic Cameras. Available online:
http://data.london.gov.uk/datastore/package/tfl-live-traffic-cameras
(Last retrieved 17/11/2012)

London JamCams application for iOS, Sendmetospace

The other notable transport dataset which has been released in June 2011 is "Cycle Hire availability".[184] First of all, bike locations could be found through a special web-site, on which in its turn all the mobile applications are based.[185]

The mobile apps, based on this dataset could help

---

[184] The official website of the London Datastore, Cycle Hire availability . Available online: http://data.london.gov.uk/datastore/package/cycle-hire-availability (Last retrieved 17/11/2012)

[185] The official website of the Transport for London, Barclays Cycle Hire / Map. Available online: https://web.barclayscyclehire.tfl.gov.uk/maps (Last retrieved 17/11/2012)

users to find the closest cycle hire location and even indicate the number of free bicycles on it.

London Bike iOS application, Big Ted Ltd

Off-line maps are preloaded and allow to observe around 400 fixed-site bike stations in the city. It is especially useful in cases when internet access is not available. This situation can happen with a citizen when he or she is on the metro (London tube) or has no internet access included in his mobile operator tariff plan, for example. Preloaded maps are provided by OpenCityMap (crowd sourcing project, voluntary based) and free to exploit by apps developers and users of the applications (citizens in this case).[186] The full potential of these kinds of mobile apps could be explored on-line. GPS capabilities of smart phones allow to navigate through the city and locate Cycle Hire stations nearby. Some versions of these mobile apps are provided with a timer, which indicates when the free hire period (30 min) is about to finish and also count approximate price of using a bike after the free hire period.

Almost all presented mobile applications require a sustainable internet connection to provide services really fast and up-to-date. This is the essence of the Smart Urban Mobility. Anyhow, some of the services as maps or timetables are also available off-line and should be preloaded.

Finally, we would also like to mention the distinction of the "London Case" as really focused on the mobile apps issues. Obviously, some web-services exist as well, but the number and diversity of apps, designed explicitly for mobile phones are making the case unique in its pure nature of urban mobility. In this case study #1 we had no aim to compare the "London Case" with two other cases, but would like to emphasize that it's the only story out of three we are looking at (London, Berlin, Brussels), which is based first of all,

---

[186] OpenCityMap project. Available online: http://www.openstreetmap.org/ (Last retrieved 08/09/2012)

purely on open data, and second, on open data initiatives specifically for mobile phones.

CASE STUDY №2. Berlin

The public transport system

Berlin is the capital of Germany and its largest city, with a population of 3,460,725 inhabitants.[187] The German capital has a widespread public transport system, which is mostly operated by BVG (or "Berliner Verkehrsbetriebe") and S-Bahn Berlin GmbH (a branch of the Deutsche Bahn) which administrates city train S-Bahn. Basically, the Berlin transportation system is Verkehrsverbund Berlin-Brandenburg (VBB), the main function of which in its turn is to control the common fare structure in the city of Berlin and also the federal state of Brandenburg.[188] This diversification is quite important to understand the mechanism of the mobility in the capital. This is why we will return to it later on.

According to resent research, the number of private transport in the German capital is quite low: 358 cars per 1000 residents, while the average in the country is 570 cars per 1000 residents. It means, that the public transport services, car-sharing initiatives and using of bicycles are quite

---

[187] The official website of Berlin, Pressemitteilungen des Landes. Available online: http://www.berlin.de/landespressestelle/ (Last retrieved 18/11/2012)
[188] The official website of Verkehrsverbund, Berlin-Bradenbourg, VBB-Fahrinfo. Available online: http://www.vbb.de/de/index.html (Last retrieved 18/11/2012)

popular ways of urban mobility (according to the same research, there are around 710 bicycles per 1000 residents).[189] To reduce harmful pollutants in the air the Environmental Zone was established in Berlin from the beginning of 2008. This zone is a special area in the German capital where only transport that meets certain exhaust emission standards is allowed to drive. Transport with particularly high emissions (mostly private transport) must stay outside the area. The boundaries are identical with the boundaries of the S-Bahn line.

Green Zone(Umweltzone), Berlin

---

[189] Neumann, P. (2012) Die Hauptstadt des umweltfreundlichen Verkehrs, Berliner Zeitung, 11/08/2009. Available online: http://www.berliner-zeitung.de/archiv/nur-ein-drittel-der-wege-legen-die-berliner-im-auto-zurueck-die-hauptstadt-des-umweltfreundlichen-verkehrs,10810590,10658688.html (Last retrieved 04/11/2012

Legislative framework
PSI Directive implementation

By of 13 December 2006 the PSI Directive[190] (DIRECTIVE 2003/98/EC OF THE EUROPEAN PARLIAMENT AND OF THE COUNCIL on the re-use of public sector information (of 17 November 2003)) was transposed to the German national law by adopting explicit PSI re-use measures and launching a new legislative instrument: *"Gesetz über die Weiterverwendung von Informationen öffentlicher Stellen (Informationsweiterverwendnugsgesetz - IWG)*[191] The IWG regulates both – the Federal and the municipal administrative level.[192]

According to the English translation of the document,

---

[190] EUROPEAN PARLIAMENT & COUNCIL (2003) DIRECTIVE 2003/98/EC OF THE EUROPEAN PARLIAMENT AND OF THE COUNCIL on the re-use of public sector information (of 17 November 2003), *Official Journal of the European Union* Available online: http://eur-lex.europa.eu/LexUriServ/LexUriServ.do?uri=OJ:L:2003:345:0090:0096:EN:PDF (Last retrieved 12/06/2012)

[191] Der Bundestag (2006) Gesetz über die Weiterverwendung von Informationen öffentlicher Stellen, Bundesgesetzblatt Jahrgang. Available online: http://ec.europa.eu/information_society/policy/psi/docs/laws/germany/new_law_dec_2006.pdf (Last retrieved 18/11/2012)

[192] Vandenbroucke, D. & D. Biliouris (2010) "Spatial Data Infrastructures in Germany: State of Play 2011". Available online: http://inspire.jrc.ec.europa.eu/reports/stateofplay2011/rcr11DEv132.pdf (Last retrieved 17/11/2012)

made by the internal services of the European Commission, there is no exact list of existing public-sector bodies in the territory of the country. Thus, public-sector bodies can be defined as: *" a) state, regional and local authorities, including their special assets; b) other legal persons governed by public or private law established for the specific purpose of meeting needs in the general interest, not having an industrial or commercial character, for the most part financed by the bodies referred to under (a) or (c) either individually or jointly, by participation or otherwise, or whose management is supervised by these bodies, or more than half of the members of whose management or supervisory organs are appointed by these bodies. The same shall apply where the body that for the most part finances, either individually or jointly with other bodies, or appoints, either individually or jointly with other bodies, more than half of the members of the management or supervisory organs, falls under the first sentence; c) associations whose members fall under (a) or (b);"* [193]

Furthermore, according to the national transposition legislation, a *public sector body may charge for giving a right to re-use*, but not exceeding marginal costs of collection, production, reproduction and dissemination of data. A non-discrimination policy and prohibition of exclusive arrangements stated in the

---

[193] The European Commission official website, INSPIRE Monitoring & Reporting. Available online: http://inspire.jrc.ec.europa.eu/index.cfm/pageid/182/list/indicators/y/2011/sel/2 (Last retrieved 17/11/2012)

PSI Directive are transposed to the German PSI legislation.

In February 2012 the paper **„Berliner Open Data-Strategie"**[194] was launched as a result of collaboration between the local government and researchers from Fraunhofer FOCUS Institute. The paper emphasizes the role of The Berlin Data Portal, which is supposed to be a platform between the State of Berlin and its citizens (apps developers as well): *"The collected data sets are machine readable and freely licensed, and therefore enable greater transparency of administrative procedures and provide, for example, information about infrastructural and environmental aspects in the city and encourage further use and processing by third parties...The portal currently offers access to about 60 data sets in 15 different data categories not only of public authorities but already also of other organizations."*[195] It is also said that the

---

[194] Florian Marienfeld (2012) Berlin Open Data Strategy, English abstract of the report „Berliner Open Data-Strategie", Fraunhofer FOCUS. Available online: http://epsiplatform.eu/sites/default/files/BerlinerOpenDataStrategy_english_abstract.pdf (Last retrieved 18/11/2012). Full Document in German: http://www.berlin.de/projektzukunft/fileadmin/user_upload/pdf/sonstiges/Berliner_Open_Data-Strategie.pdf

[195] Florian Marienfeld (2012) Berlin Open Data Strategy, English abstract of the report „Berliner Open Data-Strategie", Fraunhofer FOCUS, pp. 3-5. Available online: http://epsiplatform.eu/sites/default/files/BerlinerOpenDataStrategy_english_abstract.pdf (Last retrieved 18/11/2012). Full Document in German: http://www.berlin.de/projektzukunft/fileadmin/user_upload/pdf/sonstiges/Berliner_Open_Data-Strategie.pdf

users may use the data from the portal for any purposes under the license "Creative Commons Attribution 3.0 Germany" (CC BY).

This paper explicitly explaines a "step-by-step plan" for the "Berlin Open Data strategy", which includes short-, medium- and long-term measures. First of all, in the short-term period, open data has to be integrated into the local administrative regulations of the State of Berlin and the Berlin data portal has to be up-dated on a regular basis. The medium-term perspective provides a sustainable development of the data services of the German capital. According to this measure, added-value services and necessary trainings should be provided. Finally, in the long-term period for "Berlin Open Data strategy", the pan-national coordination and integration of the Berlin data services into services of Germany and the German-speaking countries and in Europe should be developed.

In fact, Berlin is the first German city which started to allow public access to its datasets. The information is available to citizens, businesses and academic institutions, journalists, and other interested groups. Ideally, the portal should provide Berliners with more transparency and possibilities.

INSPIRE Directive implementation

The governmental structure in Germany has three individual levels: local, regional and national. Each level generates and holds public information including geo-spatial data. As a result, this complicated structure is influencing the development of the German data initiatives. Therefore, good coordination of work and cooperation between the federation, Federal States and municipalities is essential. Thus, the document *"Geodatenzugangsgesetz"* [196] was published in 2008 aiming to implement the INSPIRE Directive[197] at the Federal level in Germany. The document creates a legal framework to access spatial data, spatial data services and metadata from the Federal geodata owners.

At state level a number of state agencies keep geo-

---

[196] Deutscher Bundestag (2008) Drucksache 16/10530, "Entwurf eines Gesetzes über den Zugang zu digitalen Geodaten (Geodatenzugangsgesetz – GeoZG)", Gesetzentwurf der Bundesregierung. Available online: http://dip21.bundestag.de/dip21/btd/16/105/1610530.pdf (Last retrieved 18/11/2012)

[197] EUROPEAN PARLIAMENT & COUNCIL (2007) DIRECTIVE 2007/2/EC OF THE EUROPEAN PARLIAMENT AND OF THE COUNCIL establishing an Infrastructure for Spatial Information in the European Community (INSPIRE) (of 14 March 2007), *Official Journal of the European Union*. Available online: http://eur-lex.europa.eu/LexUriServ/LexUriServ.do?uri=OJ:L:2007:108:0001:0014:EN:PDF (Last retrieved 08/06/2012)

spatial datasets. To fill the information gap between different territories, these agencies were involved in the design of the German spatial data catalogue.[198] This catalogue included selected metadata information from federal and state governments. The plan for now is to supply and standardize geo-spatial data and services on a national German basis in order to meet the specifications of the INSPIRE Directive.[199]

According to the administration agreement between Federal and State governments on data exchange, the federal and state governments should provide each other with mutual access to the basic environmental data (not necessarily by opening it up for a third parties).[200] Furthermore, according to this document, state authorities authorize the Federal government to make non-commercial use of geo-spatial data for the official national and

---

[198] Vandenbroucke, D. & D. Biliouris (2010) "Spatial Data Infrastructures in Germany: State of Play 2011". Available online: http://inspire.jrc.ec.europa.eu/reports/stateofplay2011/rcr11DEv132.pdf (Last retrieved 17/11/2012)

[199] EUROPEAN PARLIAMENT & COUNCIL (2007) DIRECTIVE 2007/2/EC OF THE EUROPEAN PARLIAMENT AND OF THE COUNCIL establishing an Infrastructure for Spatial Information in the European Community (INSPIRE) (of 14 March 2007), *Official Journal of the European Union*. Available online: http://eur-lex.europa.eu/LexUriServ/LexUriServ.do?uri=OJ:L:2007:108:0001:0014:EN:PDF (Last retrieved 08/06/2012)

[200] Vandenbroucke, D. & D. Biliouris (2010) "Spatial Data Infrastructures in Germany: State of Play 2011". Available online: http://inspire.jrc.ec.europa.eu/reports/stateofplay2011/rcr11DEv132.pdf (Last retrieved 17/11/2012)

international purposes.

Finally, towards the INSPIRE Directive implementation a number of tasks are still have to be completed[201]:

- adoption of Federal Law and by the State laws.
- implementation of spatial-data Network
- participating on in European geo-spatial data initiatives
- creation of common architecture concept and interoperability

As we may see, apart from the Berlin strategy, the open data reality in the country is not so prominent at the moment. Germany implemented the PSI Directive in December 2006 with a Federal law (IWG), but the local political situation, administrative structures and legislation are very different compared with most of the other EU member states. As an example – there is no central office of PSI (public sector information). This makes it a challenge indeed for PSI re-use in Germany to find out who has the legal competence to open up the data, since Germany is a

---

[201] Vandenbroucke, D. & D. Biliouris (2010) "Spatial Data Infrastructures in Germany: State of Play 2011", p. 19 Available online: http://inspire.jrc.ec.europa.eu/reports/stateofplay2011/rcr11DEv132.pdf (Last retrieved 17/11/2012)

Federation comprising 16 Federal States with great autonomy in generating, managing and publishing PSI.

On the other hand, if we look at the "bottom-up" situation, we see recent changes. During the last Berlin state election, which was held on 18 September 2011, the Pirate Party Germany (*Piratenpartei Deutschland*) got 8.9 percent of the vote. The party is focused on Internet freedoms, open source governance and digital privacy issues as well as free urban transportation. [202] According to „Berliner Open Data-Strategy" launched In January 2012, these particular elections have shown that people of Berlin are more and more claiming for an open governmental system and free access to databases as part of this system. This report also shows that in 2010 around 88% of the German capital citizens were *"strongly in favor of non-personal information being made public by the public authorities and 81% of them considered this to be a chance for more participation".* [203]

---

[202] The official website of the Pirate party in Germany, Piratenpartei Deutschland. Available online:
http://www.piratenpartei.de/politik/ (Last retrieved 08/06/2012)
[203] Florian Marienfeld (2012) Berlin Open Data Strategy, English abstract of the report „Berliner Open Data-Strategie", Fraunhofer FOCUS, pp. 3-5. Available online:
http://epsiplatform.eu/sites/default/files/BerlinerOpenDataStrategy_english_abstract.pdf (Last retrieved 18/11/2012). Full Document in German:

Overview of applications for urban mobility in Berlin

The VBB (Verkehrsverbund Berlin-Brandenburg) provides citizens with real-time information. The timetables and route planning functions are available on-line for all digital devices of Berlin citizens and tourists. Depending on the producer and/or the platform of the device, mobile phones, tablets and PC can work with the system getting the off-line (time schedules) and real-time information. The use of telephone call requests is also possible in order to obtain the route and public transport information. It is especially useful for those citizens who have no smartphones or internet access on their mobile devices. Since the beginning of 2011 it is also operated by an automatic voice-dialogue system.[204]

FahrInfo is one of the mobile apps which is based on the VBB route planner, but created by third-party developers. Basically, every private user (for example a Berlin citizen or a

---

http://www.berlin.de/projektzukunft/fileadmin/user_upload/pdf/sonstiges/Berliner_Open_Data-Strategie.pdf

[204] The official website of Verkehrsverbund, Berlin-Bradenbourg, VBB-Fahrinfo. Available online: http://www.vbb.de/de/index.html (Last retrieved 18/11/2012)

guest of the city) can use VBB route planner for her or his own needs for free. It means that the desktop version of the planner is available on the official web site of the organization. FahrInfo developers (Metaquark)[205] are using the same data from VBB. The app is based on XML version of the VBB Route Planner. On the iTunes page of the application, the developers are warning users, that this public transport app is not actually an official one and it is only based on the data provided by VBB.[206]

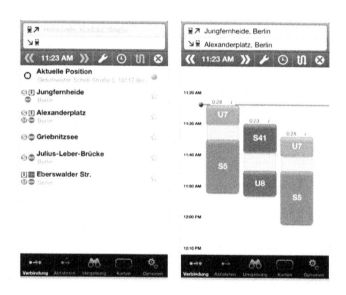

FahrInfo Berlin iOS application, Metaquark

---

[205] The official website of Mttaquark, software company. Available online: http://metaquark.de/.
[206] iTunes, FahrInfo application. Available online : https://itunes.apple.com/fr/app/fahrinfo-berlin/id284971745?mt=8 (Last retrieved 18/11/2012)

Can we say that VBB is providing developers with open data? Going back to the theoretical Chapter on "Open Data", we can refer to the "5-stars" typology[207] of Berners-Lee and will conclude that it is not open data. The reason why is that the data, available on the web-site *is not interoperable and not machine-readable*. Moreover, the mobile apps based on the VBB route planner are free for citizens, but web-developers need to pay for using the data provided by VVB). The transport organization obliges developers to sign a usage agreement that requires attribution and profit sharing if a developer makes a certain amount of money per year.

Basically, the data for this app is coming from the public governmental sources. Usage is allowed with attribution to the source. All data are provided in the not machine-readable format. Which means they are not "Open Data" in the classical sense because of the propriety format. The data are open but not easy to process.

One more application, available for iOS and Android platforms, is *DB Navigator* developed by Deutsche Bahn itself (or one of it sub-developers).

---

[207] Berners-Lee, T. (2010) Speech on "Open, Linked Data for a Global Community", *Gov 2.0 Expo 2010*. Available online: http://www.youtube.com/watch?feature=player_embedded&v=ga1aSJXCFe0 (Last retrieved 17/11/2012)

DB Navigator application for Android, Deutsche Bahn AG

The application is free and presented in German and English. Deutsche Bahn is the only owner and re-user of the data they have, the company is not ready to open these data to third parties. Even though Deutsche Bahn is the national corporation and is owned by the Federal Republic of Germany.[208]

---

[208] The official website of Deutsche Bahn, Deutsche Bahn AG at a glance. Available online:

During our research we also have found some mobile apps, created for cyclists in Berlin (see Appendix). In general, these apps are nothing but the off-line maps more or less specifically tailored for bicycle routes. They have the options to show the user's location through the GPS system on the smart phone and count the distance passed. Anyhow, these types of apps don't use any real-time information as for example an indication of the nearest bike-parking or showing the number of available bikes.

Another application, which in our opinion deserves to be mentioned in the "Berlin Case" is the project *"Mapnificent"*, a desktop application, based on GTFS (The General Transit Feed Specification by Google, which defines a common format for public transportation schedules and geospatial data).

---

http://www.deutschebahn.com/en/group/ataglance/facts_figures.html (Last retrieved 18/11/2012)

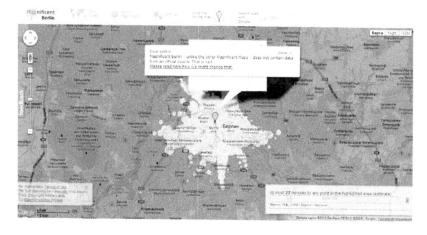

Desktop application Mapnificent

As it is written on the web-site of the application *"Mapnificent shows you the area you can reach with public transport from any point in a given time."*[209] Basically, it means that a user can choose any street or any particular building on this street, set a time parameter and figure out which area can be covered by the public transport with the given time. For example, how far a citizen can move away from the Brandenburg Gate by public transport in 15 minutes. The application can be useful for fast city navigation. Even though it works only in a desktop regime, it attracts around 12 000 unique visitors a month. The application can be used not only for Berlin, but for some other European and Non-European cities. Again, it is based on unofficial data: *"Dear Visitor, Mapnificent Berlin –*

---

[209] The official website of the desktop application Mapnificent. Available online: http://www.mapnificent.net/berlin

unlike the other Mapnificent Maps – does not contain data from an official source. That is sad".[210]

The lack of various mobile apps for urban mobility based on open data by local authorities has forced Berlin residents to be creative. Enthusiastic citizens invent some alternative ways of collecting the data – crowd sourcing, more specifically – they use a special *Twitter account*. At least there are two Twitter accounts: *@SBahnBerlin* (the official Twitter account of DB S-Bahn Berlin) and *@s_bahn_berlin* (unofficial account for the retweets of the passengers).

@SBahnBerlin, **Twitter account of DB S-Bahn Berlin**

---

[210] The official website of the desktop application Mapnificent, Drop me on the map. Available online
http://www.mapnificent.net/berlin/#/?lat0=52.525592&lng0=13.36954 5000000016&t0=15

@s_bahn_berlin, unofficial Twitter account for Berliners

Each has around 8000-10 000 followers, who also update information about traffic jam in the capital and sometimes provide it with pictures.

The "Open Data" initiative is relatively new for Germany. Nonetheless there are some efforts to develop it. Recently the competition "Apps4Germany"[211] was launched. The project was initiated by three German NGOs: Open Data Network, Open Knowledge Foundation, Government 2.0 Network and supported by the Ministry of the Interior Affairs. About 25.000 Euro was available as prize money, provided by sponsors. The entry deadline for applications was at the 1 February 2012, and the award session was set up in the middle of March 2012. The contest commission was representing people from the German government, civic

---

[211] The official website of the project "Apps4Germany". Available online: http://apps4deutschland.de/

organizations, academical institutions and business industries. Around 320 data sets were released by governmental structures for the competition. 112 ideas for re-use of these data were created and exactly 77 applications were launched.

The German capital is a member of the "Open Cities project", which is co-founded by the EU and aimed to promote Open and User Driven Innovations approach across the member cities (Amsterdam, Barcelona, Berlin, Helsinki, Paris, Rome, Bologna)[212]. It is remarkable that the „Berliner Open Data-Strategy"[213], which we discussed earlier in this Chapter, was launched as a result of the collaboration between the local city government and researchers from Fraunhofer FOCUS Institute, exactly under the "Open Cities project".[214]

Finally, we can say that even though the local transport companies of the German capital are not yet ready

---

[212] The official website of Open Cities project. Available online: http://opencities.net/ (Last retrieved 18/11/2012)

[213] Florian Marienfeld (2012) Berlin Open Data Strategy, English abstract of the report „Berliner Open Data-Strategie", Fraunhofer FOCUS. Available online: http://epsiplatform.eu/sites/default/files/BerlinerOpenDataStrategy_english_abstract.pdf (Last retrieved 18/11/2012) Full Document in German: http://www.berlin.de/projektzukunft/fileadmin/user_upload/pdf/sonstiges/Berliner_Open_Data-Strategie.pdf

[214] The official website of Open Cities project, Open Data Toolset Berlin. Available online: http://opencities.net/node/20 (Last retrieved 18/11/2012)

to share their data with other stakeholders, the citizens of Berlin are creative enough to search for their own smart mobility solutions (crowdsourcing, "scraping" data from the official route planner, off-line maps development). The local authorities apparently are ready to work towards opening up the public sector information. Developing open data strategy for Berlin and a participation in the EU smart cities projects can be a strong proof of this intention.

CASE STUDY №3. Brussels

The public transport system

The public transport system in the capital of Belgium is operated by the transport company STIB-MIVB [215](*Société des Transports Intercommunaux de Bruxelles / Maatschappij voor het Intercommunaal Vervoer te Brussel*). All the local trams, buses and metro lines in 19 communes of the Brussels Capital Region are administrated under this organization and all the citizens and city visitors can use a single ticket for traveling.

The two other public transport companies also operate in the city: De Lijn[216] (Flanders region) and TEC Group[217] (Wallonia region). Both organizations perform locally in two regions of the country connecting them with the capital of Belgium. In fact, both companies are organizational bodies, under authorities of which several private companies are working. STIB-MVIB ticket does not apply to these two public transport operators, as well as they themselves have separate ticket systems.

---

[215] The official website of STIB-MIVB. Available online: http://www.stib.be/index.htm?l=fr
[216] The official website of De Lijn. Available online: http://www.delijn.be/en/index.htm
[217] The official website of TEC Group. Available online: http://www.infotec.be

The National Railway Company of Belgium - NMBS/SNCB (*Nationale Maatschappij der Belgische Spoorwegen / Société Nationale des Chemins de fer Belges*) is also operating in the Brussels region. NMBS/SNCB is a national operator, whose aim is to connect different Belgian cities rather than provide services explicitly inside the City of Brussels. The same status is applied for De Lijn and TEC Group services. Thus, as long as we are looking only to the capital city case, our main focus will be on the functioning of the first mentioned public transport company - STIB-MIVB, rather than on the national operators. However, a research on the national mobility issues can be a logical extension of this case study research.

Additionally, it is useful to mention that already a few years in a row the City of Brussels local authorities organize a "Car free day".[218] Normally, it is a Sunday. Only taxis, regular city transport (buses, trams, metro) and city services (police, emergency cars, fire trucks etc.) are allowed to drive. The whole Brussels Region is closed for private car traffic from 9 am till 7 pm. Citizens may use bicycles. The public transport is often free of charge during the "Car free day".

---

[218] The official website of City of Brussels, Mobility Week and Car Free Sunday 2012. Available online: http://www.brussels.be/artdet.cfm?id=4843&agendaid=750 (Last retrieved 05/10/2012)

Legislative framework
PSI and INSPIRE Directives implementation

In this part of the Chapter we would like to combine the analysis of the both relevant Directives transpositions, because obviously in both cases there are the same issues, making the process of the implementation difficult.

The country of Belgium has a very specific and complex territorial, social, political and economical structure. First of all, there are 3 official languages in the country (as a result, all legislation is translated into Dutch, French and German). Secondly, any access to governmental information is under the territorial competences and ruled by different legislation (Brussels Capital region, Flanders, Wallonia). It makes the process of any EU policy implementation complex. In spite of it, according to the Article 32 of the Constitution of Belgium, access to the documents held by public bodies is a constitutional right since 1994: *"Ieder heeft het recht elk bestuursdocument te raadplegen en er een afschrift van te krijgen, behoudens in de gevallen en onder de voorwaarden bepaald door de wet, het decreet of de regel bedoeld in artikel 134."* (in Dutch) or *"Chacun a le droit de consulter chaque document administratif et de s'en faire remettre copie, sauf dans les cas et conditions fixés par la loi, le décret ou la règle visée à l'article 134"* (in French). [219]

Thus, the **PSI Directive** was finally transposed to all the levels, in different time though: [220]

- in the national law in March 2007,
- in Wallonia and the German communities in December 2006,
- in the Flemish community in April 2007
- the latest territory in Belgium, transposed the PSI Directive was the region of Brussels, in March 2008.

The Federal and all the regional authorities have also transposed the **INSPIRE Directive** *"with regard to the data sets and services for which they are competent"*. [221] All the Belgian authorities have signed an Agreement creating a special Coordination Committee to transpose the Directive. The

---

[219] DE BELGISCHE GRONDWET/LA CONSTITUTION BELGE (1994) Article 32. Available online:
http://www.senate.be/doc/const_nl.html (in Dutch) and
http://www.senate.be/doc/const_fr.html (in French)

[220] Janssen, K. (2011) PSI in Belgium: a slow journey towards open data? Topic Report No. 2011/1, European Public Sector Information Platform. Available online:
http://epsiplatform.eu/sites/default/files/Topic%20Report%20Belgium.pdf

[221] Vandenbroucke, D. & K. Janssen (2011) Spatial Data Infrastructures in Belgium of play 2011, K.U.Leuven. Available online:
http://inspire.jrc.ec.europa.eu/reports/stateofplay2011/rcr11BEv102.pdf
(Last retrieved 18/10/2012)

Committee is composed of two representatives from each Belgian region and two from the Federal state. The paper was adopted on 2 April 2010 and will enter into force once all the stakeholders adopt their legislation in the line with the Agreement. The Brussels Region has published its approval in April 2011. The other regions still have their documents to be published.

Thus, the current situation is unclear. There is no single legislation for the spatial data infrastructure at the Federal level, while there are separate documents in every Belgian region: the Flemish region, in Brussels, the Walloon region and the German community.[222]

Overview of applications for urban mobility in the City of Brussels

Open Data initiative in Belgium

The Open Data initiative has started in Belgium in 2009, when a student and young web-developer Yeri Tiete (see expert interview in the Appendix) created a simple

---

[222] Vandenbroucke, D. & K. Janssen (2011) Spatial Data Infrastructures in Belgium of play 2011, K.U.Leuven, p. 52. Available online: http://inspire.jrc.ec.europa.eu/reports/stateofplay2011/rcr11BEv102.pdf (Last retrieved 18/10/2012)

mobile application, which allowed seeing Belgian train schedules. He proposed this app to the Belgian National Train Authority (NMBS) with explanation of the possible business model behind (advertising opportunities). After a while the developer got the answer that his activity is actually a copyright violation and that the railway company is going to sue him if he is going make this application available on-line. The young web-enthusiast did not agree and in 2011 founded his own start-up - non-profit organization – *iRail*. Now this organization works for the promotion of open public transport data initiatives and the organization of open data events as "Apps For Ghent"[223] and "Apps For Flanders".[224] Also iRail works in Living labs domain: starts all sorts of new projects and support them to become a spin-off. They also work closely with another non-profit organization - Open Knowledge Foundation.

Looking at the current situation with Belgian open data development, it's easy to be confused and lost in all the available web-recourses, which all are supposed to be official governmental platforms.

One of the first initiatives was the web-site

---

[223] The official website of the project "Apps For Ghent". Available online: http://appsforghent.be/
[224] The official website of the project "Apps For Flanders". Available online: http://appsforflanders.be/

http://psi.belgium.be, launched in 2003, in line with the PSI Directive and actively promoted by then Flemish Minister of ICT Vincent Van Quickenborne. [225] At that time the initiative was rather new and the team of the Minister was motivated to support the project. Currently, the data sets and PSI news on the portal are updated irregularly in a nonsystematic manner. Not all of the existing data are available for free of charge or under a standard license. Some of the datasets are protected under the conditions imposed by each data provider.

The next initiative came up later, in 2011. The main initiator was the Flemish government - *http://data.gov.be*. On this website federal and Flemish public sector information data sets are made available and regularly updated. Clearly, the recourse covers only a part of the country – Flemish community and the City of Brussels to some extent.

The next existing open data portal is *http://www.openbelgium.be*. This website is a private initiative and doesn't officially cooperate with any

---

[225] Personal blog of Vincent Van Quickenborne. Available online: http://www.vincentvanquickenborne.be/blog/2011/09/overheid-bundelt-waterval-aan-informatie-op-open-data-website/#disqus_thread (Last retrieved 18/11/2012)

governmental body. The website was launched as an open platform for any public or private organization, which is ready to share its data.

Additionally, some Belgian cities have their own open data portals as for example *http://data.gent.be/* for Ghent or *http://opendata.bruxelles.be* for Brussels.

Looking at this whole range of websites and the projects behind them, it is easy for a researcher to be confused. As it was mentioned early, the legislative open data framework is still unclear (there is no single legislation for the spatial data infrastructure at the Federal level). Thus, there is not one clear national "Open Data for Belgium" initiative, even though - *http://data.gov.be* is pretending to be national, the lead is evidently Flemish.

As long as the Belgian Open Data initiative is mostly driven by the Flemish community, we find it necessary to mention the City of Ghent as the center of data activism in the country.

Referring to expert interviews with three Belgian representatives of Open Data initiative (**Geert Mareels**, coordinator of "Citadel on the move", **Bart Rosseau**, coordination expert of "e-Strategy for Ghent" and **Pieter Colpaert** – OKF activist), we came to the conclusion that the center of all Open Data activity in the country is Ghent. Ghent was the 1st Belgian city which decided to open-up it's governmental data in April 2011. [226] For 1 day governmental bodies risked to open-up their data sets to see what can be done with it. The initiative was so successful, that after this event local public authorities just kept data open.

On September 14th 2012, the Open Knowledge Foundation, together with IBBT, Flemish Government, iRail, iDrops and Multimedia Lab, organized "Apps For Flanders"[227] hackathon for students and all the open data enthusiasts. The next cities, participating in this initiative are going to be Antwerp and Leuven.

Explaining the growth of open data Belgium we also find it important to underline the "Citadel on the Move" project.[228] In the line with the Digital Agenda for Europe, Citadel on the Move was launched in 2010 and it's aimed to engage citizens over 200 cities across the globe to create new mobile applications in the areas of transportation and tourism. In other words, the project is designed to develop citizen-generated 'smart city' mobile applications that can be

---

[226] The official website of City of Ghent, Openbaarheid bestuur. Available online: http://www.gent.be/open (Last retrieved 22/11/2012)
[227] The official website of "Apps For Flanders" project. Available online: http://appsforflanders.be/.
[228] The official website of "Citadel on the Move" project. Available online: http://www.citadelonthemove.eu/

potentially used and shared in any European city. Remarkably enough this project is coordinated by the Flemish eGovernment Authority (CORVE) under the direction of the Minister for eGovernment and Tourism (the Consortium: partners from five European Countries - Belgium, France, Greece, Portugal and the United Kingdom).

Recently Brussels, the capital of Belgium, also joined the initiative of Ghent and has started to open up its data. From 24th February 2012, the website of the City of Brussels has opened the amount of datasets with short description to each. At the moment, around 30 datasets are published by cities authorities.

List of the open datasets in the City of Brussels[229]:

- Open data comic book route
- Open data French-language libraries
- Open data Dutch-language libraries
- Open data toilets
- Open data urinals
- Open data parking lots
- Open data parking space for disabled
- Open data sports halls and stadiums

---

[229] The official website of City of Brussels, Open Data. Available online: http://www.brussels.be/artdet.cfm/7254.

- Open data ATMs
- Open data Administrative centre and liaison offices
- Open data tourist offices
- Open data youth hotels
- Open data police stations
- Open data parks
- Open data cultural places
- Open data museums
- Open data French-language schools
- Open data Dutch-language schools
- Open data community centres
- Open data dog toilets
- Open data glass containers
- Open data European institutions
- Open data wifi
- Open data public computer rooms (PCRs)
- Open data Public Internet access points
- Open data Administratel terminals
- Open data municipal news
- Open data contests
- Open data job offers
- Open data invasive exotic plants
- Open data sectors of the local resident card

Datasets are available in French and Dutch and supposed to be updated monthly, quarterly, semi-annually or annually depending on every particular case. All the datasets are open under the specially created license.[230] According to the document, all the available datasets can be used for non-commercial as well as for commercial purposes and after downloading datasets the users gets a permission to "share, modify and freely use public data" without distorting the meaning of the information.

The website provides online forms where every user can propose to open up a dataset. After a proposal is examined by the city's authorities, a new dataset can become available on the website.[231]

Concerning the mobility issues, there are only 2 out of 30 datasets available:

- Open data parking lots

---

[230] City of Brussels (2012) Licence for the use of public information Brussels: a digital city. Downloaded from: http://www.brussels.be/artdet.cfm/7191 (Last retrieved 22/11/2012)
[231] The official website of City of Brussels, Suggestion for open data. Available online: http://www.brussels.be/artdet.cfm/7254.

- Open data parking space for disabled people

The official web portal provides citizens with information about parking facilities locations. The number of total and free places for each parking lot is indicated. Noticeable: parking lots in Brussels are managed by private companies, thus tree companies are in the list. Later in this Chapter we will discuss mobile apps for city parking, based on the available datasets.

Remarkable is that the list of datasets does not contain any transport information, provided by local public transport companies. STIB-MVIB owns the data (both offline schedules and real-time data) and is obviously not ready to open it up. However, it's important to note that even though in case of STIB-MVIB the transport data are closed, the mobile application allowing citizens to plan their routes exist for iOS and Android free of charge.

Overview of applications

The official mobile application based on STIB-

MIVB[232] is available for free for Android, iOS as well as a web-service. With the help of the app, a user can see when the next bus/tram/metro is departing in real-time. Permanent timetables and the function of localization are also available. The application via the function of geolocalization on the smartphone is able to determine current location of a user and suggest the nearest public transport stops.

STIB mobile application, STIB-MIVB

Moreover, STIB-MIVB has two official Twitter accounts: one for buses and metro and the other one for trams. Both accounts are conducted in French.

---

[232]The official website of STIB-MIVB, Real-time mobile information STIB information begins on my smartphone. Available online: http://www.stib.be/realtime_gsm.html?l=en

@tramstib, Twitter account of STIB-MIVB tram

@STIBMIVB, Twitter account of STIB-MVIB tram

Furthermore, STIB-MIVB signed an agreement with Google (Google Transit) to link transport data with Google maps: « *Ce partenariat entre Google et la STIB offre une vitrine incroyable à la mobilité en transports publics à Bruxelles. En effet, 40% des visiteurs du site stib.be y accèdent via un moteur de recherche et 96% d'entre eux utilisent celui proposé par Google* ». [233]

---

[233] The official website of STIB-MVIB, La STIB sur Google Transit. Available online: http://www.stib.be/google_transit.html?l=fr

STIB-MIVB on Google Transit

Practically, it means that a public sector company opened up its data exclusively to a third party, which contradicts to the Article 11 of PSI Directive: *"The re-use of documents shall be open to all potential actors in the market, even if one or more market players already exploit added-value products based on these documents. Contracts or other arrangements between the public sector bodies holding the documents and third parties shall not grant exclusive rights."*[234]

According to our data base results (see Appendix), applications in the "city guide tour" are quite popular among developers. These kinds of applications often contain off-line

---

[234] EUROPEAN PARLIAMENT & COUNCIL (2003) DIRECTIVE 2003/98/EC OF THE EUROPEAN PARLIAMENT AND OF THE COUNCIL on the re-use of public sector information (of 17 November 2003), *Official Journal of the European Union*, Article 11. Available online: http://eur-lex.europa.eu/LexUriServ/LexUriServ.do?uri=OJ:L:2003:345:0090:0096:EN:PDF (Last retrieved 12/06/2012)

maps of Brussels. It is remarkable that not only Belgians, but developers from all over the world create free and paid apps for Brussels. Perhaps, it can be explained by popularity of Belgium and the EU capital among tourists and, as a result, market request for these apps.

As it was mentioned before, the City of Brussels has opened up a number of datasets, including the information about parking lots. Thus, a few applications based on these data are available for iOS and Android. These kinds of applications are equipped with a function of geolocation, which allows identifying a current place of a user and finding the nearest parking, indicating the number of available places. We have not found any independent developers, using these data sets to create applications, but technically it is possible.

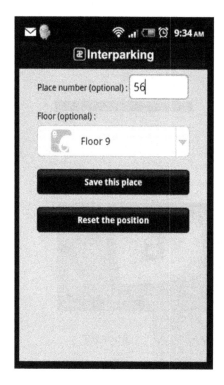

Interparking mobile app, Interparking

Augmented reality is also one of the existing mobile applications, available for free for users in Brussels.[235]

---

[235] The official website of "Brussels Augmented Reality" application. Available online: http://www.ab-arts.be/portfolio/brusselsreality/

Augmented Reality, AB Arts

The principle of application is following: focusing a smartphone camera on the specially created image (e.g. on the paper or PC monitor), it is possible to create additional pop-up data. The application can be helpful for urban mobility and terrain navigation. The application is developed by a private company and is still in the process of testing.

Final cases conclusions

1. Comparing three European cases we can obviously see how the open data initiative is spreading around the chosen territories with two different approaches: *"bottom up"* in Brussels and Berlin and *"top down"* in the City of London. While the British capital authorities are implementing special tailored programs to provide citizens with smart mobility solutions, Belgian enthusiasts and German researchers together with the national Pirate Party are working on opening up their local datasets. In both cases it is leading by organizing "hackatons" competitions, where local developers and local authorities can be involved.

2. At this period of time, the United Kingdom, and particularly the City of London, are the European leaders in open data implementation. The initiative is getting special attention from central and city governments by launching and applying in practice governmental programs and agreements as *"Smarter Government"*, *"The UK Location Programme"*, *"Public Sector Transparency Board"* and *"Open Data White Paper"*. Practically it is reflected in common interoperability standards, common web-infrastructure and regular data update. On the contrary, the idea of "Open Data" is fairly new in Germany and Belgium, as the first steps have been

taken in both countries in 2012, while in the UK the initiative has been developed since 2008. Nevertheless, the local authorities are ready to work towards opening up the public sector information. Developing an open data strategy for Berlin, open licensing in Brussels and the organization of developers competitions can be a strong proof of this intention.

3. In all three cases citizens and community are encouraged to create and develop new PC and mobile applications or to improve already existing government mobility services. The major principal difference is that in the London case it can be any person, who has skills to download and process data to create a new service. In Brussels and Berlin, local authorities cautiously open up the mobility datasets for special occasions (e.g. developers competitions, hackatons) and clearly only for specific target groups of developers, excluding ordinary citizens. In Brussels though some other relevant datasets are available online under the free for non-commercial and commercial re-use license.

4. Open data initiatives are performed in the UK at both levels - national and city level, while in Berlin and Brussels' cases it is still an issue due to the complex system of national governance in both cases. The Brussels and Berlin cases are similar in government and policy structures

complexity, which obviously slow down innovations. Additionally, both cases (Brussels and Berlin) have mobile public transport applications, launched by public bodies themselves, without giving access to data to third parties. In the Brussels case the access to the real time data is given to one single partner – Google Transit, which contradicts the EU law (PSI Directive).

5. The strong point of the London case is that all the data is collected on one single official web recourse, which is well maintained and regularly updated. It makes data more reliable. Again, due to the complex federal and national structures in Germany and Belgium, finding one reliable open data portal still remains a problem. On top, the Belgian initiative is mostly driven by the Flemish community, so the Walloon part of the country is rather excluded from benefiting the PSI access.

6. When citizens and users have no access to the transport and mobility public sector information (PSI), they are starting to be creative (or even "smart citizens"), using some alternative ways of "Smart Mobility" through the means off-line maps based applications, crowdsourcing and social networks (Twitter). All the 19 London smart mobility applications, presented in our data base, are built up on open governmental data, while in Berlin and Brussels we could not

find any open data based app for urban mobility. Instead of that "smarter citizens" took a lead on the urban mobility. On the one hand, limited access to governmental data and PSI inhibits the development of new city services, on the other hand – this fact gives room for alternative urban mobility initiatives (crowdsourcing, social networks, linked data, etc..). This *"bottom up"* approach is positively in line with the conception of "Smart City as a Creative City", which was discussed in earliest Chapters.

Conclusions and future work

Cities are becoming bigger and less comfortable. Public authorities have two basic choices when choosing a city development policy: keep expending the urban area even bigger, or make it smarter. The aim of this book was to explore how the second choice can be practically done in the specific domain of "Smart Mobility" and how city data can play its role.

1. The "smartness" of a city can be defined in different ways. A human component, reflected in the activity and creativity of citizens and policy as well as the entrepreneurship component are important factors for defining a smart city. Thus the triangle of *"Technology-People-Government"* is becoming a strong basis for a modern and intelligent city where ICT is the core element. Urban areas are making the effort to become "smarter", but they are in the very premature stage, so it is too early to judge.

2. A city, which is tending to become "smarter", should have both – real and on-line infrastructures. The way of looking at the city as at the "system of systems" is giving a perspective to distinguish two parallel essential layers of modern urban mobility: a real infrastructural layer with roads, transport and parking facilities and a virtual one, based on

ICT and data development. Infrastructure ideally should be created with the aim to make the citizen's interaction with the government more effective. Smart Mobility solutions, functioning in both layers (infrastructural and online), should first of all resolve the issue of "multimodality" when citizens use more than one transport per day. Combination of public and private services is an important part of smart mobility. Hence, Smart mobility ideally is a kind of networked mobility.

3. "Smart Mobility" is a crucial component of a "Smart City", as long as it affects all the stakeholders, from city inhabitants to the local business. Sustainable or "smart" mobility is a sum of three essential components: *social inclusion* (when all the residents regardless of social status, age, gender, physical conditions are able to be mobile in the city), *friendly environment* (reducing air and noise pollution and minimizing traffic flows through integrated urban and traffic planning) and *economy promotion* (better logistics, improving the efficiency of transit companies). It is important to keep in mind that not all of the citizens use mobile apps. Not all of them even have smartphones. Hence, an integrated approach should be implemented and some alternative ways for urban mobility should be available (SMS, real time information displays at bus stops etc.). Moreover, crowdsourcing can be an excellent tool to make citizens more mobile and at the same time

encourage people to contribute of each other's mobility.

4. Every day a modern city generates and collects a lot of data. All this amount of data can become a prominent driving force in increasing urban mobility through ICT technologies. Providing transport information can actively assist people in changing their daily movement actions. So, public data can play a significant role in a smart mobility development. We can assume that these data can create added social and economic value, especially if it's linked and combined with other public data resources.

5. The meaning of "Public Sector Information" (PSI) should not be mixed up with the meaning of "open data". They are not necessarily synonyms especially when PSI is stored by governmental services and not opened up for the other stakeholders as citizens, commercial and non-commercial organizations. Anyhow, PSI and open data definitions can overlap and even be identical in situations where public sector information is under the open access.

6. "Public sector information" and "open data" are good raw material for ICT urban development. Numerous useful services increasing the comfort of urban mobility can be based on data, collected by a city. In some cases, official authorities can share this data with third parties, giving them room for imagination and innovation. This sharing can also

stimulate governmental transparency and economical efficiency of a city. Even so, when a government is opening up its data, the degrees of openness can easily fluctuate from "complete openness" to "selective openness". Cases where local authorities keep public sector data closed are clearly presented in Europe.

7. The governmental attitude to the question of sharing public sector data affects the approach which cities takes in a development perspective: *"top down"* or *"bottom up"*. According to the first one, official authorities are supporting legislatively the public data re-use. By establishing some additional helping tools they motivate citizens and developers to freely take advantage out of it. On the contrary, following the "bottom up" approach, a government has a rather passive or even defensive position in sharing its data. It can result in discriminatory data policy when the access is exclusively open only to a single or few stakeholders. Then it is difficult to call PSI open. In such a situation, people or "smart citizens" in their turn are starting to be pro-active, demanding public data to be open, or simply finding alternative ways of making their city mobile.

8. To follow the trends, to regulate cities' mobility and the ICT impact on mobility issues and promote the best practices across the Member States, the EU institutions are

setting up legal and conceptual initiatives containing some general rules. The EU institutions have a strong opinion, that public sector information (including geographical and public transport data) should be opened and available cross-borders. This idea has been supported on a legislative level since the launching of PSI Directive in 2003. The document promotes the idea of re-using and sharing data free of charge or at least not exceeding the marginal costs. The PSI Directive is mainly based on economic reasons and the potential values of re-using public sector information for the Member States economy, while the INSPIRE Directive (2007) promotes the significance of interoperability of data within the EU. According to both documents, re-using of public data is a basis for a digital age, thus data shall be re-usable and interoperable across the EU borders. Anyhow, the last decision and time frames are up to Member States. Finally, they decide what, and in which form, national information can be open.

9. Opening up city datasets is increasing democratic control and political participation of citizens, pushing law enforcement and fostering services and product innovations. Essentially, re-use of data allows a city to function more efficient and the costs are rather low, because data have already been collected for other primary purposes of the city.

Even more: in some cases new web-services are able not only to save city's money, but also to create a new economic value for citizens. Nevertheless, the idea of opening-up and re-using public sector information is not a neutral one. Some researchers are biased, arguing that radical openness may result in unpleasant accidents and an even further lack of trust to the government. It is a relatively new phenomenon, so further independent academic and applied researches are needed.

Recommendations

After making conclusions we can now come up with valuable recommendations for the future. What can be improved in the European cities and how can they become more mobile in a "smarter open data" way?

1. First of all, it is always preferable for a city to have a single open data portal. A strong point of the London case is that all the data are collected on one single official web recourse, which is well maintained and regularly updated. It makes data more reliable. Again, due to the complex federal and national structures in Germany and Belgium, finding one reliable open data portal still remains a problem due to state structures.

2. The "data owner" and the "decision-maker" are natural gatekeepers of the urban mobility. A government or some separate governmental structures (e.g. public transport body) can be these gatekeepers. While they are deciding if data can be opened or not, they actually shape the way a city is becoming "smarter". If citizens and, more specifically, developers can not get the information they need, they will create an alternative way to get it. Sometimes it can be half-legal "scraping" of data from timetables or using any other tools. Official info is more reliable anyway. If official

authorities want to avoid data sharing or they are worried the safety of it, they need to make an analysis "pro's and cons" and find a balance. If citizens and the community have access to city data and they are encouraged to create and develop new PC and mobile applications, they can feel more trust to the government. Moreover, they can simply improve existing government mobility services for free. There are both strategic and practical benefits.

3. It is important for every European city or region to create their unique programs on open data and mobility, considering their specific state structures. For example, in the cases of Berlin and Brussels, national and regional governmental bodies have their own data autonomy. It has to be considered.

4. Smart Mobility is not only about open data. Alternative ways as crowdsoursing platforms and social networks can be successfully used and combined with open data. Then it is a perfect and very flexible model because citizens can rely on many sources and even contribute.

5. It is helpful to start an initiative from at least one city in the country, not necessarily from the capital one. The other country regions can embrace the initiative later.

6. Real time information is always more useful for

mobility than some off-line maps, which are also helpful, but actually only replace an old-fashioned paper version. Interactive maps and real-data apps operate in new mobility dimensions, making a citizen really mobile, connected and up-to-date. Additionally, it makes sense to rely on mobile phone apps rather than on desktop applications, again for reasons of faster mobility in the urban space movements.

7. City authorities should keep in mind that by giving an exclusive data access to only one or a few partners, they pursue a discrimination policy and contradict to the Article 11 of PSI Directive (non-exclusive right to PSI). On the one hand it can be enough for a small city to have only one official route planner, but on the other – there is no room for innovation.

8. Open licenses policy with attribution to the official recourse can be beneficial for both parties: developers and government. For developers, a license gives a confirmation of reliability of provided data, and for a government it creates extra trust from the citizens' community (prove that government is transparent).

9. The EU institutions should probably take more coordination responsibilities, promote the idea of data sharing across the borders and actively impose common

interoperability standards, common web-infrastructure and regular data updates.

Epilog

We sincerely believe that this book based on academic approach is a scientifically and socially relevant piece of research, because it explains the recent concept of "Smart Cities" from both a theoretical and empirical angles and it explicitly maps the role of data in the development of the concept. Not so much research has been done on this domain so far. We can see it from the lack of academic literature on the topic and very fragmented empirical research around the globe. Moreover, we believe that we succeeded in combining a theoretical framework with strong EU policy analysis and case studies research, which created a realistic picture of smart mobility in Europe.

Nevertheless, we believe that there is no limit for perfection, especially in the ICT domain research, where every day something new is coming up on conceptual, technical or legislative levels. Our research was restricted by a very specific domain, even though the general topic of smart cities is much broader. Hence, we find it interesting to continue and to deepen the research.

The other characteristics of a smart city (as "Smart People", "Smart Environment", "Smart Economy" etc.) can be better discovered. Again, the question of PSI and open data implementation to these particular characteristics can be traced. The problem of "inclusion-exclusion" of citizens in the smart mobility discourse as well as positive and negative effects of re-using public sector information also can be a good contribution to the academic research. An economic value of PSI and business modeling for open data could also be discussed in future work. There is definitely room for further promising theoretical and empirical research in this exciting domain.

About the Author

Maria SASHINSKAYA

- Journalist and open data researcher,
- EU Open Innovation 2.0 Yearbook contributor (Available here: https://ec.europa.eu/digital-single-market/news/open-innovation-20-yearbook-2013)

Twitter: @sashinskaya
BBC Russian: www.bbc.com/russian

If you enjoyed the book, please consider leaving an Amazon Review, so more readers can discover it.

Bibliography

Berners-Lee, T. (2010) Speech on "Open, Linked Data for a Global Community", *Gov 2.0 Expo 2010*. Available online: http://www.youtube.com/watch?feature=player_embedded&v=ga1aSJXCFe0 (Last retrieved 17/11/2012)

Brown, G. (2010) Speech of the Prime Minister on Building Britain's Digital Future, London. Available online: http://webarchive.nationalarchives.gov.uk/+/number10.gov.uk/news/speeches-and-transcripts/2010/03/speech-on-building-britains-digital-future-22897 (Last retrieved 03/06/2012)

Bührmann, S. & F. Wefering, S. Rupprecht (2011) Guidlines: Developing and implementing a sustainable urban mobility plan, Munich, pp. 6-15. Available online: http://www.mobilityweek.eu/fileadmin/files/docs/SUMP_guidelines_web0.pdf (Last retrieved 13/11/2012)

Cabinet Office of the UK (2012) Open Data White Paper: Unleashing the Potential. Available online: http://www.cabinetoffice.gov.uk/sites/default/files/resources/CM8353_acc.pdf (Last retrieved 17/11/2012)

California Institute for Smart Communities (2001) Smart Communities Guide Book. Available online: http://www.smartcommunities.org/guidebook.html (Last retrieved 04/08/2012)

City of Brussels (2012) License for the use of public information Brussels: a digital city. Downloaded from: http://www.brussels.be/artdet.cfm/7191 (Last retrieved 22/11/2012)

City of Hamilton (2011) Notice of Motion, *Open Data*

Policy. Available online: http://www.hamilton.ca/NR/rdonlyres/E6C548DD-2FE2-4D21-AF65-B24A2C8BEF2B/0/Aug09EDRMS_n197439_v1_10_1__Notice_of_Motion__Open_Data_Polic.pdf (Last retrieved 01/11/2012)

City of Stuttgart (2009) *Agenda 21 for Urban Mobility*, pp. 6-40.

Curtin, D.& A. Meijer (2006) "Does Transparency Strengthen Legitimacy? A Critical Analysis of European Union Policy Documents", *Information Polity*, 11(2006), pp. 109-122.

D. J. Cook & M. Youngblood (2004) "Smart Homes",. Berkshire Encyclopedia of Human-Computer Interaction. Berkshire Publishing Group.

DE BELGISCHE GRONDWET/LA CONSTITUTION BELGE (1994) Article 32. Available online: http://www.senate.be/doc/const_nl.html (in Dutch) and http://www.senate.be/doc/const_fr.html (in French)

Deloitte Consulting and Deloitte & Touche (2000) At the Dawn of e-GOVERNMENT: The Citizen as Customer. Available online: http://www.egov.vic.gov.au/pdfs/e-government.pdf (Last retrieved 10/11/2012)

Der Bundestag (2006) Gesetz über die Weiterverwendung von Informationen öffentlicher Stellen, Bundesgesetzblatt Jahrgang. Available online: http://ec.europa.eu/information_society/policy/psi/docs/laws/germany/new_law_dec_2006.pdf (Last retrieved 18/11/2012)

Deutscher Bundestag (2008) Drucksache 16/10530, "Entwurf eines Gesetzes über den Zugang zu digitalen Geodaten (Geodatenzugangsgesetz – GeoZG)",

Gesetzentwurf der Bundesregierung. Available online: http://dip21.bundestag.de/dip21/btd/16/105/1610530.pdf (Last retrieved 18/11/2012)

Directorate General for the Information Society (2000) Commercial Exploitation of Europe's Public Sector Information: Final Report. Available online: http://ec.europa.eu/information_society/policy/psi/docs/pdfs/pira_study/commercial_final_report.pdf (Last retrieved 05/07/2012)

Dutra, M. (2011) Dangers of Open Government Data, *The Networked Society Blog*. Retrieved from: http://thenetworkedsociety.blogspot.be/2011/03/dangers-of-open-government-data.html

Eaves, D. (2010) How Governments misunderstand the risks of Open Data, Personal Blog. Retrieved from: http://eaves.ca/2010/10/06/how-governments-misunderstand-the-risks-of-open-data/ (Last retrieved 04/11/2012)

EUROPEAN COMMISSION (2003) Proposal for a DIRECTIVE OF THE EUROPEAN PARLIAMENT AND OF THE COUNCIL, Amending Directive 2003/98/EC on re-use of public sector information Available online: http://ec.europa.eu/information_society/policy/psi/docs/pdfs/directive_proposal/2012/en.pdf (Last retrieved 08/06/2012)

EUROPEAN COMMISSION (2008) *Citizens summary on the Green Paper "Towards a new culture for urban mobility"*, Available online: http://ec.europa.eu/transport/themes/urban/urban_mobility/green_paper/doc/2008_citizen_summary.pdf (Last retrieved 13/11/2012)

EUROPEAN COMMISSION (2009)

COMMUNICATION FROM THE COMMISSION TO THE EUROPEAN PARLIAMENT, THE COUNCIL, THE EUROPEAN ECONOMIC AND SOCIAL COMMITTEE AND THE COMMITTEE OF THE REGIONS Re-use of Public Sector Information – Review of Directive 2003/98/EC –2009/2011)

EUROPEAN COMMISSION (2011) Legislative proposal 2011/0430(COD) - 12/12/2011. Available online: http://www.europarl.europa.eu/oeil/popups/summary.do?id=1181131&t=d&l=en (Last retrieved 06/11/2012)

EUROPEAN COMMISSION. COM (2010) 245 final. Communication from the Commission to the European Parliament, the Council, the European Economic and Social Committee and the Committee of the Regions, a Digital Agenda for Europe. 19.5.2010. Available online: http://eur-lex.europa.eu/LexUriServ/LexUriServ.do?uri=COM:2010:0245:FIN:EN:PDF (Last retrieved 15/09/2012)

EUROPEAN COMMISSION. COM(2007) 551 final. GREEN PAPER Towards a new culture for urban mobility. 25.9.2007. Available online: http://eur-lex.europa.eu/LexUriServ/LexUriServ.do?uri=COM:2007:0551:FIN:EN:PDF (Last retrieved 11/11/2012)

EUROPEAN COMMISSION. COM(2009) 490 final. COMMUNICATION FROM THE COMMISSION TO THE EUROPEAN PARLIAMENT, THE COUNCIL, THE EUROPEAN ECONOMIC AND SOCIAL COMMITTEE AND THE COMMITTEE OF THE REGIONS Action Plan on Urban Mobility, 30.9.2009. Available online: http://eur-lex.europa.eu/LexUriServ/LexUriServ.do?uri=COM:2009:0490:FIN:EN:PDF (Last retrieved 11/11/2012)

EUROPEAN PARLIAMENT & COUNCIL (2003)

DIRECTIVE 2003/98/EC OF THE EUROPEAN PARLIAMENT AND OF THE COUNCIL on the re-use of public sector information (of 17 November 2003), *Official Journal of the European Union* Available online: http://eur-lex.europa.eu/LexUriServ/LexUriServ.do?uri=OJ:L:2003:345:0090:0096:EN:PDF (Last retrieved 12/06/2012)

EUROPEAN PARLIAMENT & COUNCIL (2007) DIRECTIVE 2007/2/EC OF THE EUROPEAN PARLIAMENT AND OF THE COUNCIL establishing an Infrastructure for Spatial Information in the European Community (INSPIRE) (of 14 March 2007), *Official Journal of the European Union.* Available online: http://eur-lex.europa.eu/LexUriServ/LexUriServ.do?uri=OJ:L:2007:108:0001:0014:EN:PDF (Last retrieved 08/06/2012)

EVPSI/LAPSI (2012) Web streaming of the 4th LAPSI Internal Conference and EVPSI/LAPSI Final Meeting (9th/10th July 2012). Retrieved from: http://www.lapsi-project.eu/streaming

Fioretti, M. (2011)" Open Data: Emerging trends, issues and best practices", *Laboratory of Economics and Management of Scuola Superiore Sant'Anna,* Pisa

Florian Marienfeld (2012) Berlin Open Data Strategy, English abstract of the report „Berliner Open Data-Strategie", Fraunhofer FOCUS. Available online: http://epsiplatform.eu/sites/default/files/BerlinerOpenData Strategy_english_abstract.pdf (Last retrieved 18/11/2012). Full Document in German: http://www.berlin.de/projektzukunft/fileadmin/user_uploa d/pdf/sonstiges/Berliner_Open_Data-Strategie.pdf

Florida, R. (2002) *The Rise of the Creative Class: And How It's Transforming Work, Leisure, Community and Everyday life.* New York: Basic Books. Available at: http://www.washingtonmonthly.com/features/2001/0205.fl

orida.html (Last retrieved 05/08/2012)

Fornefeld, M. & G. Boele-Keimer, S. Recher, M. Fanning (2008) "Assessment of the Re-use of Public Sector Information (PSI) in the Geographical information, Meteorological Information and Legal Information Sectors", Final report, *MICUS Management Consulting GmbH*, Düsseldorf. Available online: http://ec.europa.eu/information_society/policy/psi/docs/pdfs/micus_report_december2008.pdf (Last retrieved 01/11/2012)

Foth, M. (Ed.) (2009). "Navigation Becomes Travel Scouting: The Augmented Spaces of Car Navigation Systems", *Handbook of Research on Urban Informatics: The Practice and Promise of the Real-Time City*. Hershey, PA, pp. 230-241

Foth, M. (Ed.) (2009). "WikiCity: Real-time location-sensitive tools for the city", *Handbook of Research on Urban Informatics: The Practice and Promise of the Real-Time City*. Hershey, PA, p. 397

Geographic Information Panel (2008) *Report to Baroness Andrews, Minister for Geographic Information Panel*, Communities and Local Government. Available online: http://location.defra.gov.uk/wp-content/uploads/2009/12/uk-location-strategy.pdf (Last retrieved 17/11/2012)

Gibson, D.V., G. Kozmetsky, R.W. Smilor, (1992) *"The Technopolis Phenomenon: Smart Cities, Fast Systems, Global Networks"*. Boston: Rowman and Littlefield Publishers

Giffinger, R. & C. Fertner, Kramar, H. Kalasek, R. Pichler-Milanovic, E.Meijers (2007) Smart Cities: Ranking of European Medium-Sized Cities, Research Report, Vienna University of Technology, Available online: http://www.smart-cities.eu/download/smart_cities_final_report.pdf (Last retrieved 22/08/2012)

Grava, S. (2003) Urban Transportation Systems: choices for communities, McGraw-Hill, Incorporated, New York, pp. 5-13

Group of authors (2010) Data, data, everywhere, *The Economist*, Special Report, Feb 25, 2010. Available online: http://www.economist.com/node/15557443 (Last retrieved 04/11/2012)

Hall, R. E. (2000). "The vision of a smart city. In Proceedings of the 2nd International Life Extension Technology" Workshop (Paris, France, Sep 28). Available online: http://www.osti.gov/bridge/servlets/purl/773961-oyxp82/webviewable/773961.pdf. (Last retrieved 11/07/2012)

Harrison, C. & B. Eckman, R. Hamilton (2010) Foundations for Smarter Cities. *IBM Journal of Research and Development*, 54(4).

Harvey, D. (1989) *From Managerialism to Entrepreneurialism: The Transformation in Urban Governance in Late Capitalism*, Geografiska Annaler. Series B, Human Geography, 71(1), The Roots of Geographical Change: 1973 to the Present, pp. 3-17.

Hollands, R.G. (2008) Will the real smart city please stand up?. In: *City*, 12(3).

Huijboom, N. & T. Van den Broek (2011) "Open data. an international comparison of strategies", *European Journal of ePractice*, 12 (March/April 2011), pp. 4-15. Available online:
http://www.epractice.eu/files/European%20Journal%20epractice%20Volume%2012_4.pdf (Last retrieved 15/08/2012)

iTunes, FahrInfo application. Available online: https://itunes.apple.com/fr/app/fahrinfo-berlin/id284971745?mt=8 (Last retrieved 18/11/2012)

Janssen, K. (2011) PSI in Belgium: a slow journey towards open data? Topic Report No. 2011/1, European Public Sector Information Platform. Available online: http://epsiplatform.eu/sites/default/files/Topic%20Report%20Belgium.pdf

Koetsier, J. (2012) An operating system for cities: How IBM plans to make your city smarter, VentureBeat. Available online: http://venturebeat.com/2012/06/29/ibm-city-operating-system/ (Last retrieved 13/11/2012)

Komninos, N. (2002) *Intelligent Cities*. London: Spon Press

Kroes, N. (2010) *"The critical role of cities in making the Digital Agenda a reality"*, Closing speech to Global Cities Dialogue Spring Summit of Mayors Brussels, 28 May 2010

Kroes, N. (2012) Speech on ePSI conference in Rotterdam March 2012. Available online: http://www.youtube.com/watch?v=9Jq4Qy1UeAE (Last retrieved 03/11/2012)

Kronenburg, T. (2011) "Differences in the 2008 and 2010 public online consultations regarding the PSI Directive", Topic Report No. 2011/8, *European Public Sector Information Platform*. Available online: http://ru.scribd.com/doc/106896070/Topic-Report-Differences-Public-Consultations (Last retrieved 06/11/2012)

Landry, C (2008) The Creative City: A toolkit for urban innovators, London: Earthscan.

Lorsignol, F. & Y. Sheri (2011) Intelligent City, 33th

Carleton University Industrial design Seminar Series.

Maura Reynolds (2009) "Open government or 'Transparency Theater?", NBS NEWS. Available online: http://www.msnbc.msn.com/id/32128642/ns/politics-cq_politics/#.UJ6dz-QsArU (Last retrieved 9/11/2012)

Murray-Rust, P. (2012) BioIT 2009 – What is data? *Personal blog on open knowledge.* Available online: http://blogs.ch.cam.ac.uk/pmr/2009/04/29/bioit-2009-what-is-data-1/ (Last retrieved 04/11/2012)

Nam T. & T. A. Pardo (2011) *"Conceptualizing Smart City with Dimensions of Technology, People, and Institutions",* The Proceedings of the 12th Annual International Conference on Digital Government Research, Center for Technology in Government University at Albany, State University of New York, U.S. Available online: http://www.ctg.albany.edu/publications/journals/dgo_2011_smartcity/dgo_2011_smartcity.pdf (Last retrieved 10/11/2012)

Neumann, P. (2012) Die Hauptstadt des umweltfreundlichen Verkehrs, Berliner Zeitung, 11/08/2009. Available online: http://www.berliner-zeitung.de/archiv/nur-ein-drittel-der-wege-legen-die-berliner-im-auto-zurueck-die-hauptstadt-des-umweltfreundlichen-verkehrs,10810590,10658688.html (Last retrieved 04/11/2012

Obama, B. (2009) "Memorandum for the Heads of Executive Departments and Agencies: Transparency and Open Government". Available online: http://www.whitehouse.gov/the_press_office/TransparencyandOpenGovernment

OECD (2004) "Declaration on Access to Research Data from Public Funding"

OECD (2007) "Principles and Guidelines for Access to Research Data from Public Funding" Available online: http://www.oecd.org/science/scienceandtechnologypolicy/38500813.pdf (Last retrieved 21/09/2012)

Open Knowledge Foundation (2012) Open Data Handbook. Available online: http://opendatahandbook.org/en/glossary.html#term-public-sector-information (Last retrieved 01/10/2012)

OpenCityMap project. Available online: http://www.openstreetmap.org/ (Last retrieved 08/09/2012)

O'Reilly, T. (2010) Government as a Platform, Lathrop, D. & L. Ruma (eds) *Open Government*, O'Reilly Media, p.11-44

Pentikousis, K. (2011) "Network Infrastructure at the Crossroads the Emergence of Smart Sities", Conference Publication on Intelligence in Next Generation Networks (ICIN), 15th International Conference, Berlin, 4-7 Oct. 2011.

Personal blog of Vincent Van Quickenborne. Available online: http://www.vincentvanquickenborne.be/blog/2011/09/overheid-bundelt-waterval-aan-informatie-op-open-data-website/#disqus_thread (Last retrieved 18/11/2012)

Rogers, S. (2011) UK government open data: good bad or dangerous? Tell us what you think, *The Guardian Data Blog*. Available online: http://www.guardian.co.uk/news/datablog/2011/aug/04/uk-government-open-data-maude (Last retrieved 01/11/2012)

Schaffers, H. & N. Komninos (2011) "Smart Cities and the Future Internet: Towards Cooperation Frameworks for Open Innovation", *The future Internet*, Springer-Verlag Berlin, pp. 431-446

Swan, A. (2012) "Policy Guidelines for the Development and Promotion of Open Access", *Published by the United Nations Educational, Scientific and Cultural Organization – UNESCO*. Available online: http://unesdoc.unesco.org/images/0021/002158/215863e.pdf (Last retrieved 21/09/2012)

The European Commission official website, INSPIRE Monitoring & Reporting. Available online: http://inspire.jrc.ec.europa.eu/index.cfm/pageid/182/list/indicators/y/2011/sel/2 (Last retrieved 17/11/2012)

The Minister for the Cabinet Office (2005) No. 1515, PUBLIC SECTOR INFORMATION

The official website of "Apps For Flanders" project. Available online: http://appsforflanders.be/.

The official website of "Brussels Augmented Reality" application. Available online: http://www.ab-arts.be/portfolio/brusselsreality/

The official website of "Citadel on the Move" project. Available online: http://www.citadelonthemove.eu/

The official website of Berlin, Pressemitteilungen des Landes. Available online: http://www.berlin.de/landespressestelle/ (Last retrieved 18/11/2012)

The official website of Berlin, Umweltzone – Aktuelles. Available online: http://www.stadtentwicklung.berlin.de/umwelt/luftqualitaet/de/luftreinhalteplan/umweltzone_aktuelles.shtml (Last retrieved 18/11/2012)

The official website of City of Brussels, Mobility Week and Car Free Sunday 2012. Available online: http://www.brussels.be/artdet.cfm?id=4843&agendaid=750

(Last retrieved 05/10/2012)

The official website of City of Brussels, Open Data. Available online: http://www.brussels.be/artdet.cfm/7254.

The official website of City of Brussels, Suggestion for open data. Available online: http://www.brussels.be/artdet.cfm/7254.

The official website of City of Ghent, Openbaarheid bestuur. Available online: http://www.gent.be/open (Last retrieved 22/11/2012)

The official website of City of London. Available online: http://data.london.gov.uk/ (Last retrieved 12/11/2012)

The official website of De Lijn. Available online: http://www.delijn.be/en/index.htm

The official website of Deutsche Bahn, Deutsche Bahn AG at a glance. Available online: http://www.deutschebahn.com/en/group/ataglance/facts_figures.html (Last retrieved 18/11/2012)

The official website of Metaquark, software company. Available online: http://metaquark.de/.

The official website of Open Cities project, Open Data Toolset Berlin. Available online: http://opencities.net/node/20 (Last retrieved 18/11/2012)

The official website of Open Cities project. Available online: http://opencities.net/ (Last retrieved 18/11/2012)

The official website of STIB-MIVB, Real-time mobile information STIB, information begins on my smartphone. Available online: http://www.stib.be/realtime_gsm.html?l=en

The official website of STIB-MIVB. Available online: http://www.stib.be/index.htm?l=fr

The official website of STIB-MVIB, La STIB sur Google Transit. Available online: http://www.stib.be/google_transit.html?l=fr

The official website of TEC Group. Available online: http://www.infotec.be

The official website of the Cabinet Office, Open Data White Paper and Departmental Open Data Strategies. Available online: http://www.cabinetoffice.gov.uk/content/open-data-white-paper-and-departmental-open-data-strategies (Last retrieved 17/11/2012)

The official website of the City of London, City transport policies. Available online: http://www.cityoflondon.gov.uk/Corporation/LGNL_Services/Transport_and_streets/Transport_policy/strategic_transport.htm (Last retrieved 17/11/2012)

The official website of the desktop application Mapnificent, Drop me on the map. Available online http://www.mapnificent.net/berlin/#/?lat0=52.525592&lng0=13.369545000000016&t0=15

The official website of the desktop application Mapnificent. Available online: http://www.mapnificent.net/berlin

The official website of the European Union (2012) Digital Agenda: Commission's Open Data Strategy, Questions & answers. Available online: http://europa.eu/rapid/press-release_MEMO-11-891_en.htm?locale=en (Last retrieved 13/08/2012)

The official website of the European Union. Available

online: http://europa.eu/ (Last retrieved 15/10/2012)

The official web-site of the French Environment and Energy Management Agency. Available online: http://www2.ademe.fr/servlet/KBaseShow?sort=-1&cid=96&m=3&catid=17585

The official website of the London Datastore, Cycle Hire availability. Available online: http://data.london.gov.uk/datastore/package/cycle-hire-availability (Last retrieved 17/11/2012)

The official website of the London Datastore, TfL Live Traffic Cameras. Available online: http://data.london.gov.uk/datastore/package/tfl-live-traffic-cameras (Last retrieved 17/11/2012)

The official website of the London Olympic Games 2012. Available online: http://www.london2012.com/making-it-happen/transport/index.php (Last retrieved 17/11/2012)

The official website of the Open Knowledge Foundation. Available online: http://okfn.org/ (Last retrieved 01/10/2012)

The official website of the Pirate party in Germany, Piratenpartei Deutschland. Available online: http://www.piratenpartei.de/politik/ (Last retrieved 08/06/2012)

The official website of the project "Apps For Flanders". Available online: http://appsforflanders.be/

The official website of the project "Apps For Ghent". Available online: http://appsforghent.be/

The official website of the project "Apps4Germany". Available online: http://apps4deutschland.de/

The official website of the Transport for London, Barclays Cycle Hire / Map. Available online: https://web.barclayscyclehire.tfl.gov.uk/maps (Last retrieved 17/11/2012)

The official website of the Transport for London, Live bus departures. Available online: http://countdown.tfl.gov.uk/#/ (Last retrieved 17/11/2012)

The official website of the Transport for London, Transport data service. Available online: http://www.tfl.gov.uk/termsandconditions/11402.aspx (Last retrieved 17/11/2012)

The official website of the UK Government, Open Data Applications. Available online: http://data.gov.uk/apps (Last retrieved 12/11/2012)

The official website of the UK Government, Open public license for PSI. Available online: http://www.nationalarchives.gov.uk/doc/open-government-licence/ (Last retrieved 10/06/2012)

The official website of the UK Government. Available online: http://data.gov.uk/ (Last retrieved 12/11/2012)

The official website of the UK Government. Local Spending Data Guidance. Available online: http://data.gov.uk/blog/local-spending-data-guidance (Last retrieved 17/11/2012)

The official website of Verkehrsverbund, Berlin-Bradenbourg, VBB-Fahrinfo. Available online: http://www.vbb.de/de/index.html (Last retrieved 18/11/2012)

The Re-use of Public Sector Information Regulations, Available online:

http://www.legislation.gov.uk/uksi/2005/1515/pdfs/uksi_2 0051515_en.pdf (Last retrieved 10/06/2012)

The United Nations (2011) "Technology Roadmap Carbon Capture and Storage in Industrial Applications", UNITED NATIONS INDUSTRIAL DEVELOPMENT ORGANIZATION

The United Nations (2007)The Millennium Development Goals Report. Available online: http://www.un.org/millenniumgoals/pdf/mdg2007.pdf (Last retrieved 13/11/2012)

The United Nations (2011) "The State of World Population 2011 Report", *the United Nations Population Fund.* . Available online: *http://foweb.unfpa.org/SWP2011/reports/EN-SWOP2011-FINAL.pdf* (Last retrieved 15/09/2012)

The US Federal Government open data web portal: http://www.data.gov/ (Last retrieved 15/10/2012)

Thomas, S. (2009) Slim City, materials of the World Economic Forum, slide 14 Available online: http://www.driversofchange.com/slimcity/downloads/urban_mobility_low_res.pdf (Last retrieved 11/11/2012)

Uhlir, P.F. (2009) "The Socioeconomic Effects of Public Sector Information on Digital Networks: Toward a Better Understanding of Different Access and Reuse Policies: Workshop Summary", *US National Committee CODATA, in cooperation with OECD.*

UK Location Programme Team (2010) "UNITED KINGDOM 2010, INSPIRE Monitoring and Reporting". Available online: http://location.defra.gov.uk/wp-content/uploads/2009/11/UK-INSPIRE-REPORT-2010-v1-3.pdf (Last retrieved 17/11/2012)

Vandenbroucke, D. & D. Biliouris (2010) "Spatial

Data Infrastructures in Germany: State of Play 2011". Available online: http://inspire.jrc.ec.europa.eu/reports/stateofplay2011/rcr11DEv132.pdf (Last retrieved 17/11/2012)

Vuchic, V. R. (1999) "Transportation for livable cities", Northwestern University, Center for Urban Policy Research, pp. 23-93

Walravens, N. (2011)"The City as a Platform: A Case based Exploration of Mobile Service Platform Types in the Context of the City", Materials of the 3rd International Workshop on Business Models for Mobile Platforms (BMMP), ICIN Conference, Berlin